Economic Analysis of MILLENNIUM DEVELOPMENT GOALS

A Case of Poverty and Hunger in India

MJP PUBLISHERS

ECONOMIC ANALYSIS OF

MILLENNIUM DEVELOPMENT GOALS

A CASE OF POVERTY AND HUNGER IN INDIA

S. RAMASWAMY

Professor, Department of Economics,
The Gandhigram Rural Institute, (Deemed University),
Gandhigram - 624 302, Tamil Nadu, India.

O.V UMMER KUTTY

Post-Graduate Teacher, Economics,
Bhavans Public School, Doha,
Qatar.

MJP PUBLISHERS

Chennai Trichy New Delhi Tirunelveli

MJP PUBLISHERS

ISBN 978-81-8094-430-7

Printed and bound in India

MJP 550

MJP Publishers
No. 44, Nallathambi Street,
Triplicane, Chennai 600 005

Publisher : **C. Janarthanan**

Project Editor : **C. Ambica**

PREFACE

Development goals are essential and pre-conditions for sustainable development for which 191 United Nations members have gathered together for the adoption of United Nations Millennium Declaration in 2000. Accordingly, countries have taken decision to achieve the following goals such as:

- eradicate extreme poverty and hunger;
- achieve universal primary education;
- promote gender and equality and empower women;
- reduce child mortality;
- improve maternal health;
- combat HIV/AIDS, malaria and other diseases;
- ensure environmental sustainability; and
- develop a global partnership for development.

These goals are aimed to be achieved by 2015. The achievement of these goals depends upon how these countries have taken up the goals seriously and sincerely. Moreover, large scale financial budgets are required to implement these goals. Financial viability and technical feasibilities of each country decide the success or failure of these goals. In this book, the authors have made sincere efforts to deal with poverty and hunger as case studies of our country. The authors hope this book will be useful to researchers and student communities in the field of economics.

The authors are thankful to MJP Publishers for showing keen interest to publish this book.

S. RAMASWAMY
O.V. UMMER KUTTY

CONTENTS

CHAPTER I

Introduction

The Millennium Declaration, was signed by 189 countries, including 147 Heads of State and Government, made during the UN Millennium Summit on 8 September 2000, and it recommended eight which are popularly called the Millennium Development Goals **(MDGs)**. According to the Declaration "every individual has the right to dignity, freedom, equality, a basic standard of living including freedom from hunger and violence and finally it encourages the tolerance and solidarity. Further MDGs projected the efforts of the international community to "spare no effort to free our fellow men, women and children from the abject and dehumanizing conditions of extreme poverty." We are now less than 600 days to the 2015 target date for achieving the MDGs. This year's report **(2014)** looks at the areas where actions are needed most. For example, one in eight people worldwide remain hungry. Too many women die in childbirth when we have the means to save them. More than 2.5 billion people lack improved sanitation facilities, of which one billion continue to practice open defecation, a major health and environmental hazards. Our resource base is in serious decline and polluted, with shrinking forests, eroding soils, collapsing fisheries, falling water tables, more destructive storms, rising sea level, disappearing species, oil spills and oil sticks, in a world already experiencing the impacts of climate change. The MDGs eight goals are further subdivided into 18 numerical targets which are further measured by means of 48 quantifiable indicators. Subsequently the targets and indicators under the 8 goals have been increased to 21 and 60 respectively (Ministry of statistics and Implementation, 2014). The objectives are specified in many different ways. Some objectives are set out in proportional terms: reducing the proportion of people who live in poverty or hunger by one-half; reducing child mortality rates by two-thirds; reducing maternal mortality rates by three- fourths; or reducing the proportion of people without access to safe drinking water and basic sanitation facilities by one-half. Other objectives are set out in terms of completion: universal primary education; gender equality in school education; productive employment with decent work for all; or universal access to reproductive health. Yet other objectives are set out as statements of intentions: reduce loss in bio-diversity or improve the lives of slum-dwellers. The eight goals are to eradicate extreme poverty and hunger, to achieve universal primary education, to promote gender equality and empowering women, to reduce child mortality rates, to improve maternal health, to combat HIV/AIDS, malaria, and other diseases, to ensure environmental sustainability to develop a global partnership for development .Among the eight goals we are concentrated on the first goal which every country want to sweep out from it's grass root level. Poverty implies a condition in which a person finds him unable to maintain a living standard adequate for his physical and mental efficiency. He even fails to meet his basic requirements.

Since the early 1950s, Government has initiated, sustained, and refined various planning schemes to help the poor to attain self-sufficiency in food production. Probably the most important initiative has been the supply of basic commodities, particularly food at controlled prices, available throughout the country as the poor spend about 80 per cent of their income on food. The schemes have however not been very successful because the rate of poverty reduction lags behind the rapid population growth rate. Eradication of poverty in India is generally only considered to be a long-term goal. Increasing stress on education, reservation of seats in government jobs and the increasing empowerment of women and the economically weaker sections of society are also expected to contribute to the alleviation of poverty. It is incorrect to say that all poverty reduction programmes have failed. The growth of the middle class (which was virtually non-existent when India became a free nation in August 1947) indicates that economic prosperity has indeed been very impressive in India, but the distribution of wealth is not at all even.

Concepts of Poverty

Absolute and Relative Poverty

Two types poverty are common in economic literature and they are: Absolute and relative. In the **absolute standard**, minimum physical quantities of cereals, pulses, milk etc. are determined in subsistence level and then the price quotations convert into monetary terms the physical quantities. Aggregating all the quantities including a figure expressing per capita consumption expenditure is determined. The population, whose level of income is below the figure, is considered to be below poverty line. According to the **relative standard**, income distribution in different fractile group is estimated and a comparison of the level of living of the top 5 to 10 per cent with the bottom 5 to 10 per cent of the population reflects the relative standards of poverty. It is very difficult to draw a demarcation line between affluence and poverty.

Poverty Headcount Ratio

Poverty headcount ratio is nothing but the ratio of the persons below poverty level income or expenditure (q/n) where q measures the population below poverty line and n measures the total population. In short, we can say it is the percentage of population below the national poverty line.

Poverty Gap Ratio

It can be defined as unity minus the average income below the poverty line to the poverty level income. Now days it is estimated from monthly per capita consumption expenditure data based on Mixed Recall Period (MRP).

Statement of the Problem

Poverty being a concrete reality affecting the Indian society for the past several decades, individual researchers and institutions has attempted from time to time to measure its extent, dimensions and have identified those sections of people affected by it. However, studies on poverty are not confined to just one discipline alone; instead, it was one of the themes of research for Sociologists and Anthropologists, apart from Economists. Essentially, the approaches followed to measure poverty differed considerably from discipline to discipline. This may be the reason why all social science disciplines, converge on the truth that the problem of poverty is of a multi-disciplinary nature having many facets. Our perspective being mainly connected with economics, a brief description of the studies carried out in India on the subject of poverty and analyse the progress towards eradicate the extreme poverty and hunger with the light of India's millennium development goals reports. Despite different achievements in India in development arena, still 350 to 400 million people remains below poverty line. So, the present study makes attempts to find out the misconceptions and mistakes made by economists including bureaucratic policy makers who involved in estimation of poverty.

The Objectives

The main objectives of the topic dealt in the book as follows:

- To understand the progress of India towards eradicating extreme poverty and hunger with light of millennium development goals.
- To examine the loopholes made by economists during the estimation of poverty.
- To suggest the policy suggestions to improve the poverty problem.

Methodology and Tools Used

The study is descriptive in nature. This is sought to analyse India's progress for achieving the first goal, that is, eradicate extreme poverty and hunger. The study relies mainly on secondary data especially with the support of various millennium development goals report in different years published by Ministry of Statistics and Programme Implementation (MoSPI), Government of India. For providing the clear picture of the Indian economy in case of poverty status, the data collected from different sources such as ministry of rural development, planning commission, ministry of agriculture, recent articles from different journals such as frontline, economic and political weekly, southern economist, economic challenger etc. and from earlier studies were used.

Period of the Study

The study was conducted during the academic year 2013-14. The secondary data collected mainly from the period of 2005 to 2014.

Scope of the Study

This study has reviewed the policy documents released and published different organizations including governments and non-profit making organizations. Reviewing and appraising the documents and reports could yield a better, at the same time socially and economically viable approaches for betterment of society in achieving the MDGs within the stipulated time. Moreover, the study of this kind could provide and identify soft paths and hard paths, the ways and means for an effective implementation of the programmes cited in MDGs

Limitations of the Study

- A difficulty faced while analyzing the secondary data was non-availability of country's report in order.
- It may not cover all the aspects of the topic mainly due the time and cost constraints.
- It is very difficult to reach in a specified conclusion because different authors and reports substantiate the differently.
- We does not know exactly how the data collection process was done and how well it was done in case of secondary data, we cannot predict the problems arise in the future
- We have no control over the data because the data are collected by someone else for some other purpose.

Chapter Scheme

The present study of the book "Economic Analysis of MDGs: A Case of Poverty and Hunger in India" The book is divided in to Five chapters. **Chapter one** gives a brief introduction about the millennium development goals, statement of the problem, the objectives, methodology and tools used, period of the study, scope and limitations of the study. **Chapter two** deals with Genesis of Millennium Development Goals and small description of each goal. **Chapter three** attempts a review of the major research studies already carried out in the area of poverty and millennium development goals. **Chapter four** presents analysis of secondary data. **Chapter five** summarizes the major findings and conclusions

CHAPTER II

Genesis of Millennium Development Goals

Introduction

In September 2000, the Millennium Declaration was adopted at the Millennium Summit, held in the framework of the 55th General Assembly of the United Nations (UN). The summit was attended by the heads of state or government of nearly all UN member states. In the wake of the Millennium Summit, a joint working group was constituted with representatives from the UN, the World Bank, the Organisation for Economic Co-operation and Development (OECD) and other international organisations. It extracted a number of measurable targets from two of the eight chapters of the Millennium Declaration – Chapter 3 "Development and poverty eradication") and Chapter 4 ("Protecting our common environment") and specified these goals by 18 targets and 48 indicators. Most of the goals are set to be implemented by 2015. In September 2001, the MDGs were approved by the 56th UN General Assembly. The international community was thus in possession of a common goal system that has been agreed upon by all relevant actors and that is both measurable and set to be implemented by a fixed date. The Millennium Development Goals (MDGs) and targets come from the Millennium Declaration, signed by 189 countries, including 147 heads of State and Government, in September 2000. The eight (8) Goals as under:

Eradicate Extreme Poverty and Hunger

The first goal, eradicate extreme poverty and hunger consists of two important targets viz. Halve, between 1990 and 2015, the proportion of people whose income is less than one dollar a day and Halve, between 1990 and 2015, the proportion of people who suffer from hunger. The two targets are again subdivided into different indicators such as Poverty Head Count Ratio **(PHCR)**, Poverty Gap Ratio **(PGR)** and Share of poorest quintile in national consumption are comes under target one. Prevalence of underweight children under-three years of age is one of the most important indicators which come under the second target. As far as India's progress towards the first goal, it is hopeful that India is on-track.

Achieve Universal Primary Education

Education is the act or process of imparting or acquiring general knowledge, developing the powers of reasoning and judgment, and generally of preparing oneself or others intellectually for mature life. It is the foremost responsibility of a society to educate its citizens. Focus should be on women's education because the knowledge and empowerment of one woman can bring about a change in a family and even the society as a whole. A person becomes perfect with education as he is not only gaining something from it, but also contributing to the growth of a nation. We must realise the importance of education. We must aim to ensure that each citizen of our nation is educated and independent. Under this goal, the main target is, to ensure that, by 2015, children everywhere, boys and girls alike, will be able to complete a full course of primary schooling with the support of three indicators such as Net enrolment ratio in primary education, Proportion of pupils starting grade 1 who reach last grade of primary and Literacy rate of 15-24 year-olds, women and men.

Promote Gender Equality and Empower Women

The MDG-framework is rooted in the recognition that gender equality and women's empowerment are vital for the realization of human rights for all. In order to achieve gender equality, it is necessary to build a society in which women and men share equally in the distribution of power and influence and have equal access to education, health, decent work and livelihoods. Two thirds of the world's illiterate adults are female and over 65% of its poorest people are women and girls **(UNDP Report 2013)**. Across the world, gender-based inequalities continue to deny women a say in the decisions that affect their lives. It focus to Eliminate gender disparity in primary and secondary education, preferably by 2005, and in all levels of education no later than 2015.It has also three indicators namely Ratios of girls to boys in primary, secondary and tertiary education, Share of women in wage employment in the non-agricultural sector and Proportion of seats held by women in national parliament.

Reduce Child Mortality

A child's risk of dying is highest in the neonatal period, the first 28 days of life. Safe childbirth and effective neonatal care are essential to prevent these deaths. According to **NFHS-II**, 44 per cent of child deaths under the age of five take place during the neonatal period. Nearly three million babies die every year in their first month of life and a similar number are stillborn. Within the first month, up to one half of all deaths occur within the first 24 hours of life, and 75 per cent occur in the first week. India has realized impressive gains in child survival over the last two decades. However, at the current pace, the country is unlikely to achieve the Millennium Development Goal (MDG) 4 -which aims to reduce Under-Five Mortality (U5MR) by two thirds between 1990 and 2015- unless the related socio-economic; maternal and demographic; and environmental determinants are urgently addressed. It concentrated on Reduce by two-thirds, between 1990 and 2015, the under-five mortality rate. It has three indicators viz., Under-three mortality rate, Infant mortality rate and proportion of 1 year-old children immunised against measles.

Improve Maternal Health

While maternal mortality is related to a variety of health, social and economic factors, the majority of deaths are directly caused by a limited number of complications such as haemorrhage, hypertensive disorders, sepsis, and obstructed labour which require access to emergency obstetric care. It targeted to Reduce by three quarters, between 1990 and 2015, the maternal mortality ratio and Achieve, by 2015, universal access to reproductive health. This goal has maternal mortality ratio, proportion of births attended by skilled health personnel, contraceptive prevalence rate, adolescent birth rate, antenatal care coverage (at least one visit and at least four visits) and unmet need for family planning.

Combat HIV/AIDS, Malaria and TB

AIDS treatment and prevention, such as intensive programmes promoting increased use of condoms, delayed sexual initiation and fewer sexual partners can reduce the rate of these deaths. WHO says one child is killed by malaria every 30 seconds. Measures such as the use of insecticide-treated mosquito bed nets and malaria control activities can turn the tide. Disease is a cruelly potent child killer, especially when combined with the poverty in which much of the developing world lives. In the absence of good nutrition, sanitation and health care, HIV/AIDS, malaria, measles, polio and tuberculosis mean certain end to millions of children who would survive and flourish elsewhere. The major targets under this goal are namely, have halted by 2015 and begun to reverse the spread of HIV/AIDS, Achieve, by 2010, universal access to treatment for HIV/AIDS for all those who need it and Have halted by 2015 and begun to reverse the incidence of malaria and other major diseases.

Ensure Environmental Sustainability

Environmental sustainability is a set of ideas and practices with a long term goal of conserving natural resources; minimizing waste, pollution, and other negative forms of human impact; and promoting global environmental and ecological awareness. The effects of environmental degradation and climate change threaten the achievement of all the Millennium Development Goals (MDGs). The poor in developing countries are especially vulnerable and the least able to adapt to the effects of environmental degradation. There have been only modest improvements and many setbacks in meeting the targets of this goal. Progress on this MDG is extremely varied both in terms of geographic region and individual targets. The main targets are Integrate the principles of sustainable development into country policies and programmes and reverse the loss of environmental resources, reduce biodiversity loss, achieving, by 2010, a significant reduction in the rate of loss, Halve, by 2015, the proportion of people without sustainable access to safe drinking water and basic sanitation and by 2020, to have achieved a significant improvement in the lives of at least 100 million slum dwellers.

Develop Global Partnership for Development

The United Nations Millennium Declaration represents a global agreement to develop further an open, rule-based trading and financial system, address the special needs of least developed countries, landlocked and small-island developing states, deal comprehensively with debt burdens for developing countries, provide access to affordable essential medicines, and increase access to new technologies .It also foster global links between the public and private sector to drive more and better development. The eighth aims holistic development of developing countries with the support of developed countries through aid, debt relief, and better opportunities for trade etc.

Among the eight goals we are concentrated on the first goal and try to elucidate the position of India towards achieving the target. We also throw a third eye on the defects faced by policy makers while estimation of poverty, implantation of programmes etc.

Eighteen (18) targets were set as quantitative benchmarks for attaining the goals. The United Nations Development Group **(UNDG)** in its 2nd Guidance note (**endorsed in 2003**) on 'Country Reporting on the Millennium Development Goals' provided a framework of 53 indicators (**48 basic + 5 alternative**) which are categorized according to targets, for measuring the progress towards individual targets. Subsequently the targets and indicators under the 8 goals have been increased to 21 and 60 respectively. The objectives are specified in many different ways. Some objectives are set out in proportional terms: reducing the proportion of people who live in poverty or hunger by one-half; reducing child mortality rates by two-thirds; reducing maternal mortality rates by three-fourths; or reducing the proportion of people without access to safe drinking water and basic sanitation facilities by one-half. Other objectives are set out in terms of completion: universal primary education; gender equality in school education; productive employment with decent work for all; or universal access to reproductive health. Yet other objectives are set out as statements of intentions: reduce loss in bio-diversity or improve the lives of slum-dwellers. Millennium Development Goals and its indicators at glance are given below (Table no.1)

Table 1.1 Official lists of MDG indicators

Millennium Development Goals (MDGs)

Goals and Targets (from the Millennium Declaration)	Indicators for monitoring progress
Goal 1: Eradicate extreme poverty and hunger	
Target 1.A: Halve, between 1990 and 2015, the proportion of people whose income is less than one dollar a day	1.1 Proportion of population below $1 (PPP) per day 1.2 Poverty gap ratio 1.3 Share of poorest quintile in national consumption
Target 1.B: Achieve full and productive employment and decent work for all, including women and young people	1.4 Growth rate of GDP per person employed 1.5 Employment-to-population ratio 1.6 Proportion of employed people living below $1 (PPP) per day 1.7 Proportion of own-account and contributing family workers in total employment

Goals and Targets (from the Millennium Declaration)	Indicators for monitoring progress
Target 1.C: Halve, between 1990 and 2015, the proportion of people who suffer from hunger	1.8 Prevalence of underweight children under-five years of age 1.9 Proportion of population below minimum level of dietary energy consumption
Goal 2: Achieve universal primary education	
Target 2.A: Ensure that, by 2015, children everywhere, boys and girls alike, will be able to complete a full course of primary schooling	2.1 Net enrolment ratio in primary education 2.2 Proportion of pupils starting grade 1 who reach last grade of primary 2.3 Literacy rate of 15-24 year-olds, women and men

Goals and Targets (from the Millennium Declaration)	Indicators for monitoring progress
Goal 3: Promote gender equality and empower women	
Target 3.A: Eliminate gender disparity in primary and secondary education, preferably by 2005, and in all levels of education no later than 2015	3.1 Ratios of girls to boys in primary, secondary and tertiary education 3.2 Share of women in wage employment in the non-agricultural sector 3.3 Proportion of seats held by women in national parliament
Goal 4: Reduce child mortality	
Target 4.A: Reduce by two-thirds, between 1990 and 2015, the under-five mortality rate	4.1 Under-five mortality rate 4.2 Infant mortality rate 4.3 Proportion of 1 year-old children immunised against measles

Goals and Targets (from the Millennium Declaration)	Indicators for monitoring progress
Goal 5: Improve maternal health	
Target 5.A: Reduce by three quarters, between 1990 and 2015, the maternal mortality ratio	5.1 Maternal mortality ratio 5.2 Proportion of births attended by skilled health personnel
Target 5.B: Achieve, by 2015, universal access to reproductive health	5.3 Contraceptive prevalence rate 5.4 Adolescent birth rate 5.5 Antenatal care coverage (at least one visit and at least four visits) 5.6 Unmet need for family planning

Goals and Targets (from the Millennium Declaration)	Indicators for monitoring progress
Goal 6: Combat HIV/AIDS, malaria and other diseases	
Target 6.A: Have halted by 2015 and begun to reverse the spread of HIV/AIDS	6.1 HIV prevalence among population aged 15-24 years
	6.2 Condom use at last high-risk sex
	6.3 Proportion of population aged 15-24 years with comprehensive correct knowledge of HIV/AIDS
	6.4 Ratio of school attendance of orphans to school attendance of non-orphans aged 10-14 years
Target 6.B: Achieve, by 2010, universal access to treatment for HIV/AIDS for all those who need it	6.5 Proportion of population with advanced HIV infection with access to antiretroviral drugs

Goals and Targets (from the Millennium Declaration)	Indicators for monitoring progress
Target 6.C: Have halted by 2015 and begun to reverse the incidence of malaria and other major diseases	6.6 Incidence and death rates associated with malaria
	6.7 Proportion of children under 5 sleeping under insecticide-treated bed nets
	6.8 Proportion of children under 5 with fever who are treated with appropriate anti-malarial drugs
	6.9 Incidence, prevalence and death rates associated with tuberculosis
	6.10 Proportion of tuberculosis cases detected and cured under directly observed treatment short course
Goal 7: Ensure Environmental Sustainability	
Target 7.A: Integrate the principles of sustainable development into country policies and programmes and reverse the loss of environmental resources	7.1 Proportion of land area covered by forest
	7.2 CO2 emissions, total, per capita and per $1 GDP (PPP)
	7.3 Consumption of ozone-depleting substances
	7.4 Proportion of fish stocks within safe biological limits

Goals and Targets (from the Millennium Declaration)	Indicators for monitoring progress
Target 7.B: Reduce biodiversity loss, achieving, by 2010, a significant reduction in the rate of loss	7.5 Proportion of total water resources used 7.6 Proportion of terrestrial and marine areas protected 7.7 Proportion of species threatened with extinction
Target 7.C: Halve, by 2015, the proportion of people without sustainable access to safe drinking water and basic sanitation	7.8 Proportion of population using an improved drinking water source 7.9 Proportion of population using an improved sanitation facility
Target 7.D: By 2020, to have achieved a significant improvement in the lives of at least 100 million slum dwellers	7.10 Proportion of urban population living in slums

Goals and Targets (from the Millennium Declaration)	Indicators for monitoring progress
Goal 8: Develop a global partnership for development	
Target 8.A: Develop further an open, rule-based, predictable, non-discriminatory trading and financial system Includes a commitment to good governance, development and poverty reduction – both nationally and internationally Target 8.B: Address the special needs of the least developed countries	Some of the indicators listed below are monitored separately for the least developed countries (LDCs), Africa, landlocked developing countries and small island developing States. **Official development assistance (ODA)** 8.1 Net ODA, total and to the least developed countries, as percentage of OECD/DAC donors' gross national income 8.2 Proportion of total bilateral, sector-allocable ODA of OECD/DAC donors to basic social services (basic education, primary health care, nutrition, safe water and sanitation)

Goals and Targets (from the Millennium Declaration)	Indicators for monitoring progress
Includes: tariff and quota free access for the least developed countries' exports; enhanced programme of debt relief for heavily indebted poor countries (HIPC) and cancellation of official bilateral debt; and more generous ODA for countries committed to poverty reduction	8.3 Proportion of bilateral official development assistance of OECD/DAC donors that is untied 8.4 ODA received in landlocked developing countries as a proportion of their gross national incomes
Target 8.C: Address the special needs of landlocked developing countries and small island developing States (through the Programme of Action for the Sustainable Development of Small Island Developing States and the outcome of the twenty-second special session of the General Assembly)	8.5 ODA received in small island developing States as a proportion of their gross national incomes **Market access** 8.6 Proportion of total developed country imports (by value and excluding arms) from developing countries and least developed countries, admitted free of duty

Goals and Targets (from the Millennium Declaration)	Indicators for monitoring progress
Target 8.D: Deal comprehensively with the debt problems of developing countries through national and international measures in order to make debt sustainable in the long term	8.7 Average tariffs imposed by developed countries on agricultural products and textiles and clothing from developing countries 8.8 Agricultural support estimate for OECD countries as a percentage of their gross domestic product 8.9 Proportion of ODA provided to help build trade capacity **Debt sustainability** 8.10 Total number of countries that have reached their HIPC decision points and number that have reached their HIPC completion points (cumulative) 8.11 Debt relief committed under HIPC and MDRI Initiatives 8.12 Debt service as a percentage of exports of goods and services

Goals and Targets (from the Millennium Declaration)	Indicators for monitoring progress
Target 8.E: In cooperation with pharmaceutical companies, provide access to affordable essential drugs in developing countries	8.13 Proportion of population with access to affordable essential drugs on a sustainable basis
Target 8.F: In cooperation with the private sector, make available the benefits of new technologies, especially information and communications	8.14 Fixed-telephone subscriptions per 100 inhabitants 8.15 Mobile-cellular subscriptions per 100 inhabitants 8.16 Internet users per 100 inhabitants

Source : *United Nations Official Website (www. un. org)*

All the eight goals, 12 out of the 18 targets and 35 indicators relating to these targets constitute India's statistical tracking instrument for the MDGs. India follows the MDGs framework accepted by the Government of India **(GoI)** which is on the basis of 2003 UNDG (**United Nations Development Group**) guidelines. Eventhough, some of the indicators which were found better suited to the Indian context were used in lieu of the specified indicators under MDGs as per UNDG framework 2003. For example under target-2, indicator 4, prevalence of underweight children under 3 years, (**instead of under 5 years**) is considered. Under target 4, indicator 9, for ratio of girls to boys in primary, secondary and tertiary education, gender parity index **(GPI of Gross Enrolment Ratio)** has been considered, under target 7, indicator 19, condom use to overall contraceptive use among currently married women 15-49 years is considered, the corresponding UNDG indicator is irrespective of age, sex or marital status. Likewise there are a few indicators which have been modified to suit Indian context. In case of some of the indicators non- availability of sufficiently reliable data is the reason for dropping them like Target 1, indicator 1, proportion of population below $1 (PPP) per day, Target 2, indicator 5, proportion of population below minimum level of dietary energy consumption. Targets 12 to 17 appearing in the UNDG framework have been dropped as these are not relevant for India. While the Goals are spelt out in general terms, the targets under these Goals specifically outline the way to achieve the Goals in a specific time frame, and the indicators under each Target are more focused and tell in concrete terms the expected level of achievements in well defined areas to be achieved in the given time frame. Some of the MDGs targets are relative to the base year (1990) value (Target- 1, 2, 5, 6, and 10) and the levels of achievement by 2015 for most of the indicators under these targets are fairly specific, and are in tune with the global targets. The other targets (Target 3,4,7,8,9,11,12) envisages either full (100%) attainment or reversal of trend, or a general improvement in living standards. MDGs have helped in bringing a much needed focus and pressure on basic development issues, which in turn led the governments at national and sub national levels to do better planning and implement more intensive policies and programmes. In India the various development programmes / schemes are formulated and implemented under the Five Year Plans (**FYP**). The 12th FYP (**2012-2017**) goal is to achieve "Faster, More Inclusive and Sustainable Growth" which is in conformity with the MDGs.

The 12th Plan has identified 25 core indicators which reflect the vision of rapid, sustainable and more inclusive growth and some of the indicators of 12th Plan are more stringent than the MDGs. The 12th Plan aims to reduce the Poverty Head Count Ratio (**PHCR**) by 10 percentage points over the preceding estimates by the end of 12th Plan, that is PHCR to be reduced to 11.9% by 2017, the corresponding MDG indicator is to reduce PHCR to 20.74% by 2015.The 12th Plan aims to reduce under-nutrition among children aged 0-3 years to half of the NFHS -3 level (that is from 40% to 20%) by the end of 12th Plan, which means by 2017. The corresponding MDG indicator is to reduce prevalence of under nutrition among children below 3 years to 26% by 2015. The 12th plan envisages reducing IMR to 25 per 1,000 live births, and reducing MMR to 100 per 100,000 live births by 2017, the corresponding MDG indicators are to reduce IMR to 27 per 1,000 live births and to reduce MMR to 109 per 100,000 live births by 2015.Coming to India's achievement in respect of the MDGs, it is a mixed bag. For some indicators India is fast, that is, it has already achieved the target level well ahead of the dead line, like halving the percentage of population below the poverty line (indicator 1A),Net Enrolment Ratio in primary education(indicator 6), proportion of people with sustainable access to an improved water sources, urban and rural (indicator 30). Target 7 and Target 8, which are of the trend reversal type, have also been realized as India has successfully halted the spread of HIV/ Aids and reversed the spread of HIV/ Aids. India has halted spread of Malaria and TB and has ensured reversal of spread of Malaria and TB.

In respect of some indicators, India is expected to reach close to the target level by 2015 if not actually meet the target level like Ratio of girls to boys in primary and secondary education and tertiary education (indicator 9), at primary level this Target has been met already, at the secondary level India will be close to achieving gender parity by 2015, but at the tertiary level it is unlikely to achieve Gender parity by 2015. In case of reducing by two-thirds the Under Five Mortality Rate (indicator 13) the U5MR is estimated at 52 per 1000 live births in 2012. To meet the Target, India has to reduce it to 42 per 1000 live births by 2015. Keeping in mind the sharp decline in U5MR witnessed during the last few years (annual reduction by 3 percentage points during the last 3-4 years) India is expected to reach very close to the target level by 2015. In the extremely crucial field of 'improving maternal health' between 1990 and 2015 India is supposed to reduce by three quarters the Maternal Mortality Ratio **(MMR)**. The latest estimate of MMR brought by the Office of RGI puts the MMR at 178 per 100,000 live births in 2012. This is a substantial improvement from an estimated MMR level of 437 per 100 000 live births in 1990-91. But India is unlikely to reach the targeted level of 109 per 100000 live births by 2015.

The areas of concern are the rest of the Indicators especially those relating to share of women in wage employment in the non – agricultural sector (indicator 11), proportion of seats held by women in National Parliament (indicator 12), proportion of population with access to improved sanitation, urban and rural (indicator 31), in respect of these indicators India is lagging behind by a huge margin.

Summary

This chapter gives the evolution of millennium development goals adopted by United Nations in September 2000. The eight goals such as Eradicate extreme poverty and hunger; Achieve universal primary education; Promote gender equality and empower women; Reduce child mortality; Improve maternal health; Combat HIV/AIDS, malaria and other diseases; Ensure Environmental Sustainability; and Develop a global partnership for development are briefly discussed in the subsequent paragraphs with the help of target pinned by each goal and its indicators. It will helps to get an overview about the eight goals and to understand it's importance among member countries.

CHAPTER III

Review and Appraisal of Literature

A diagnostic study on poverty requires an elaborate exercise of stocktaking of previous analogous contributions directed towards enriching the literature on poverty. The fact that, in the process of thematic elucidation of development economics, the concept of poverty still enjoys a pivotal place which doesn't mean that no aggressive action has been taken in the past against the already identified crucial factors compounding the intensity and severity of the problem of poverty. The over-flooded literature on poverty proves itself to be a lasting testimony to the multi-faceted and determined effort made so far to unearth those vital factors. This chapter is schematized in such a way as to obtain a three-fold classification of the available literature on poverty viz., (i) International, (ii) National and (iii) Regional levels.

International Level Studies

In a country-specific inter-temporal study on poverty from 1984/85 to 1987/88, **Malik (1993)** has revealed, through his analytical competence, the positive impacts of higher income growth in terms of real production, private income and 'public incomes' in the form of social services and infrastructure on the incidence and intensity of poverty. Inferences favour the view that trickle-down effects seem to operate in Pakistan and they strongly support the applicability of Kuznet's hypothesis. But Malik's study is weak in its approach towards framing certain policy prescriptions to redress poverty in Pakistan.

Analytical exercises on poverty carried out on an aggregate dimension by **Louise Fox et.al. (1993)** really failed in representing the pulse of the poor in Brazil. It reminds one of the facts that any realistic study on poverty should pierce the mask of superficiality to reach the depth of deprivation. But the concluding part of their analysis stresses the need for policies that would increase the efficiency of growth and hence the speed of trickle-down. The emphasis laid on growth in private formal sector and on the need to strengthen the growth potentialities of the economy as the panacea for poverty is attributed to the growth experience of Brazil prior to 1970s and during the 1980s.

The de-compositional exercise done by **Datt et.al. (1992)** to show how changes in poverty measures can be decomposed into growth and distribution components can be considered as an improvement on previous studies. Brazilian experience in combating poverty can be comfortably explained by both growth and redistribution components depending on the period under consideration. The adverse distributional effects on poverty are related to the relatively slow growth of employment in the formal sector whereas decline in mean income is associated to the recessionary phase during 1981-1983.

More or less same view emerges from an analytical study related to the evolution of the distribution of income and poverty in Brazil in the 1980s, conducted by **Ferreira et.al.(1996)** on the basis of a large and comprehensive data set from the Brazilian Statistical Office's Annual National Household Survey. Decadal changes in poverty from 1981-1990 are measured in terms of Foster-Greer-Thorbecke **(FGT)** measures. Macroeconomic instability, recessionary trends during the early 1980s and macroeconomic aggregates like unemployment, inflation, GDP change, real wages etc. are brought to the realm of discussion to analyze poverty.

Rather a sharper treatment of poverty with powerful explanatory variables is obtained from **Scott's (2000)** study on poverty mobility among small farm households in Chili over a period of 20 years. The entire study is set against the background of profound structural transformations in Chili But the gap between the periods chosen for this study is too wide to accommodate the impact of interim changes on poverty. Concluding note stresses the option that small farmers are left to the mercy of governmental benevolence alone.

An elaborate account of the possible impact of development achieved during the reform period on poverty in China is given by **Yao (2000)**. An ever-widening regional and sectoral income disparity with its positive impact on rural poverty is identified as the major disquieting feature of Chinese development experience. The extent of rural poverty is examined by confining the analysis to a conventional format with mean income and Gini co-efficients as explanatory variables. Successful fight against poverty during 1978-84 has been facilitated by both rapid growth in income and controlled income inequality whereas the picture is reversed to add to the misfortune of the poor. It is estimated that due to the slow growth of rural income compounded by declining agricultural production and failure to contain growing income inequality, China lost one decade of development efforts, to eradicate poverty between 1984 and 1995.

In an effort to account for the possible effects of common shocks such as rainfall and idiosyncratic shocks related to crops, livestock and illness on poverty transitions, **Dereon et.al. (2000)** conducted an exploratory analysis within the framework of standard inter-temporal optimization model of consumption on the basis of the survey data collected in 94-95 from Ethiopia. The regression analysis records quite remarkable responsiveness of consumption to seasonal incentives related to prices and agricultural activities and the adverse impact of shocks in agricultural activities on the capacity of households to keep consumption smooth and on the desired path. But practical suggestions for supplementing the existing safety-net (operates in the form of food-for work and food-aid distribution and registers only a relatively marginal effect on these vulnerable households) to improve the lot of these vulnerable agrarian households whose fortunes are tied to the common and idiosyncratic shocks are not forthcoming at the expected level.

In a study on 'spatial poverty traps' **Jalan et.al (1997)** implemented a regression test on farm - household panel data for rural areas of Southern China to find strong evidence of divergent impacts of geographical capital on consumption growth at the micro level. The empirical significance of 'poverty traps' is proved by the results derived from this analytical exercise which discloses that households in certain areas of rural China with poor geographical capital (physical, human and social capital) exhibit tendencies of declining consumption in comparison with their counterparts in better off areas.

Inter-sectoral and inter-temporal trends in poverty in Philippines are examined by **Balisacan (1996)** and measured by applying the PGT measures of poverty on periodically updated sectoral and regional Poverty Lines. Balisacan's views favour the income in- equalizing but poverty reducing role of agricultural growth in Philippines. Equally important status is given to demographic and socio-economic factors in shaping the destiny of rural poor households. When HDI as a better measure of human poverty is substituted for other measures of income poverty, Philippines is pushed down in the ladder of social development in comparison with its South East Asian counterparts. A comprehensive analysis of the interrelationship between distribution of operational holdings, their utilization pattern and tenancy conditions holds the result that inequality in the distribution of land a strong explanatory variable whereas tenancy bears only weak association to poverty. This study is an elaborate account of broader and possible options which, if brought effectively to implementation channel, will definitely go a long way to reduce rural poverty in Philippines. Analytical study of this nature conveys a message to the policy makers that the layer of practicality enveloping macro-economic policies can be strengthened to the desired level by micro tools.

Gooneratne's et.al (1984) work on poverty in Sri Lanka tries to document how the interaction of growth stimulants can weaken the agrarian system by generating certain income-depressants the negative impact of which will marginalize the agricultural laborers and tenants. Reformative ideas like mechanization, biochemical technology and land reform as policy prescription for attaining rapid growth in agrarian sector are extensively discussed. But it is convincingly proved with evidence that even such renovational attempts to improve the agrarian system along with decades-old welfare policies can pose threat to the weaker sections.

National Level Studies

Minhas (1974) estimated the extent of rural poverty for the period 1956-57 to 1967-68 on the basis of the distribution of private consumption expenditure available from different rounds of National Sample Survey **(NSS)**. Two poverty lines were considered, (i) A private consumption of Rs.240 (at 60-61 prices) per capita per year and (ii) Rs.200 per capita per year. On the basis of Rs.240, there was not any significant change in the number of people below poverty line for the period 1956-57 and 1967-68. The number was found to have fallen in good harvest years. On the basis of the poverty line of Rs.200, the number of people below poverty line fell more or less steadily (from 52.4 per cent in 1956-57 to 37.1 per cent in 1967-68).Out of the estimated 164 million people below the poverty line (In 1960-61), the study identified around 60 million as rural labour households. The remaining 104 million people belong to land operating (non-labour) households. A residual of about 10-15 million belonged to small land owners.

Bardhan (1969) studied the changes in the percentage of rural people below a minimum level of living for the period 1960-61 to 1968-69. By using the N.S.S consumption expenditure data, the poverty line considered was a monthly per capita expenditure of Rs.15 at 1960-61 prices. The results indicated that the percentage of rural people below the minimum level of living has significantly gone up from 38 percent in 1960-61 to 54 per cent in 1968-69. About the regional pattern, the study found (in 1967-68) more than half of the rural population below the minimum level of living in Bihar, Gujarat, Kerala, Madhya Pradesh, Maharashtra, Mysore, Orissa, Tamil Nadu, Uttar Pradesh and West Bengal. This increasing trend was noted in all the states of East India, except in Orissa. In Orissa, the rise in the percentage of poor people was relatively small and the absolute level of this percentage remained one of the highest in the country. Another finding of the study was that even in Punjab-Haryana, (the throbbing heart-land of Green revolution) an increase was there in the percentage of people below the minimum level.

Bhatty's (1969) estimate was on the basis of the National Council of Applied Economic Research Survey **(NCAERS)** for the period 1968-69. He used Sen's index of poverty and considered five poverty levels in terms of per capita annual income in 1968-69 (Rs.180, Rs. 240, Rs.300, Rs.360 and Rs.420).The study revealed that the inequality in the distribution of per capita consumption expenditure was uniformly less than the inequality in the distribution of income. Considerable variation in inequality in consumption expenditure was found in states between one occupation and another. Of the three occupation classes viz., labourers, cultivators, and non-agricultural workers, agricultural labourers were found to be the most deprived among the occupation classes. Although poverty among cultivators was found positively associated with income inequality, no such association was found in the case of agricultural labourers. The results indicated that larger farm sizes do not necessarily raise the income generating capacity of the rural economy. This was partly on account of geo-climatic factors and partly on account of the fact that the quantum of employment and wage rates is not affected by the manner in which the land is distributed.

Vaidyanathan (1968) examined the pattern of inequalities in per capita consumption levels by principal occupational, land holding categories and household size. In addition, an attempt was also made to find the inter-state variation in the degree of inequality in consumption. The necessary data were collected from the N.S.S. and the study covers the period 1960-61 to 1967-68. The poverty line considered was Rs.20 per capita consumption expenditure per month (at 1960-61 prices) and he estimated that the proportion of rural poor have gone up progressively from 59.5 per cent in 1960-61 to 60.4 per cent in 1964-65 and further to 67.8 per cent in 1967-68.The results also indicated large variations in the incidence of poverty among states. This was on account of the differences in average per capita consumption and its distribution. In addition, the pattern of land ownership was found more important than the pattern of land operation in determining the degree of consumption inequality.

Ahluwalia (1978) worked out the trends in the incidence of poverty in rural areas for 14 years covering the period 1956-57 to 1973-74 for India as a whole as well as for the individual states. The study also examined the relationship between poverty and agricultural growth. The poverty line was a consumer expenditure level of Rs.15 per person (for 30 days) at 1960-61 rural prices. The analysis was based on two alternative measures of poverty -the percentage of the rural population below the fixed poverty line and Sen's poverty Index. The estimates for all India showed marked fluctuation from time to time in the extent or incidence of rural poverty. The observed fluctuation in the incidence of poverty according to Ahluwalia reflects the real change in the severity of the poverty problem over time. A linear time trend fitted did not show any evidence for ascertaining a trend increase or decreases in rural poverty over the period as a whole. From this, he came to the conclusion that there had occurred an increase in the absolute number of people in poverty because of the growth in the rural population over the period. The time Pattern of the incidence of poverty for individual states also followed the pattern of fluctuation similar to all India. Thus, the study concluded that the incidence of poverty in rural India does not show any sustained trend over the past two decades, but only showed a pattern of fluctuation. The author observed a clear inverse relationship between rural poverty and agricultural performance. The study came to the conclusion that there had occurred some trickling down of benefits due to increases in agricultural production.

The study by **Saith (1981)** investigated the relationship between rural poverty, prices and agricultural production in India for the period 1956-57 to 1973-74 on the basis of secondary data. He observed price deviations are more important in explaining the fluctuations in the level of poverty than production deviations. The incidence of poverty displayed strong tendency to increase over time after taking into account the influence of price and production fluctuations. The findings of this study thus contradict the findings of Ahluwalia. In addition, the study revealed that price rises accentuate poverty rather more powerfully than production improvements alleviate it, while independently of the impact of both fluctuations, the incidence of poverty increases steadily over the period. The study also unfolded some of the determinants of rural poverty in India as percentage deviation of price index from trend level, percentage deviation of production index from trend level, and time trend.

Sundaram and Tendulkar (1988) have examined the inter-regional variations in the incidence of poverty and in the rate of unemployment. They also analyzed the link between poverty and unemployment for the self employed and the wage dependent households. The data base of the study was 27th and 32nd rounds of N.S.S. (1972-73 and 1977-78) relating to the all India rural population. The study reveals that the proportion of wage dependent households is the major factor explaining the inter-regional variations in the rate of unemployment. In addition, the average value of assets per household and average per capita consumer expenditure was found to be the other dominant variables contributing to the inter-regional variations in the incidence of poverty. As the rural poverty was found affected favourably by an increase in the average levels of household assets and gross cropped area and negatively by an increase in the inequality in the distribution of assets and consumption expenditure, the study concluded that growth in averages (output or income) may have positive or negative effects.

Similarly the enquiry by **Gaiha (1988)** attempted to explain the temporal/regional variations in poverty in terms of variation in agricultural output and prices. He studied the impact of village specific technological and household specific variables on poverty. He related the risk/probability of households being poor to the characteristics of the household. For this purpose he made use of the data on the Additional Rural Income Survey (1968-1970) carried out by National Council of Applied Economic Research **(NCAER)** relating to the year 1968-69. The study noticed that the village specific indicators exercised a poverty-reducing effect and the new agricultural technology beneficial to the poor. Among the household specific variables education was found to be associated with a lower risk of poverty, and the dependency burden was positively associated with poverty. The risk of poverty was seen different for different occupations and the contribution of each variable in explaining the variations in the risk of poverty also varied by occupation. The risk of poverty was more sharply reduced for cultivators than for casual labourers under the impact of new agricultural technology. The availability of credit was inversely related to the risk of poverty for business and craftsman, while this explanatory variable did not have any significant effect on the risk of poverty for cultivators. The risks for casual labour were not influenced by life cycle effects operating through variations in earnings across age groups.

Sanyal's (1988) study is largely concerned with the trends in poverty in fifteen major states and India as whole during the period 1954-55 to 1971-72. He linked the poverty line obtained on the basis of nutritional norm with the ownership holding size by using an indirect method. He assumed that household's level of living is determined by the amount of land it owns and it is an increasing function of the amount of land it owns for measuring poverty. The study revealed at the all India level, a substantial decline in the Sen's measure of poverty from 0.6 in 1954-55 to 0.55 in 1961-62 and subsequently it has increased to 0.58 in 1971-72. At the state level, an increasing trend in the incidence of poverty was observed in Bihar, Orissa, Punjab, Uttar Pradesh and West Bengal. A decreasing trend was observed in Jammu Kashmir, Rajasthan and Kerala while it is almost static in Assam. In Gujarat, Karnataka and Maharashtra, a substantial increase in the incidence of poverty was observed. Further, it was concluded that the inequality of land ownership is one of the causes of poverty.

Kurien (1980) estimated the extent of poverty (and the composition and distribution of expenditure among different size classes) in rural Tamil Nadu for the period 1957-58 to 1969-70. Using the various rounds of N.S.S. data and two widely accepted norms for the identification of the poor (on the basis of nutritionally adequate diet and minimum level of living), the study found in 1957-58 more than 50 per cent of the rural people below the poverty line. In 1969-70, it was slightly below 50 percent on the basis of the nutritionally adequate diet. On the basis of the minimum level of living over 74 percent were below the poverty line in 1957-58. Towards the end of 1960, it rose to nearly 80 percent and against declined to 73.98 percent in 1969-70.The result indicated a close association of rural poverty with little or no claims on resources. Thus he concluded that growth, even if quantitatively impressive, cannot provide the elementary needs of those who do not have any resources at their own hand. The author further added that poverty must be seen as the result of certain economic and social processes without reference to which it cannot be properly understood and analyzed.

Regional Level Studies

The study by **Parthasarathy et.al (1982)** examined the character of poverty among the rural poor in the West Godavari district of Andhra Pradesh drawing data from a sample study of "Employment and Unemployment of Rural Labour" conducted in West Godavari district for the period 1971-72. They considered two poverty lines (i) at the level of Rs.450 per capita and (ii) at the level of Rs.300 per capita. In order to examine the association between levels of poverty and other characteristics, they have constructed a two way contingency tables. The variables chosen were: (i) Possession of land (ii) average wage rate (iii) worker dependent ratio (iv) size of the family (v) presence or absence of female worker (vi) average level of employment (vii) regional variations and (viii) caste. The association was examined for landless and landed laborers. Chi-square test was adopted to examine the association between poverty and the variables mentioned earlier. The results of Chi-square test reveal that possession of land alone was found to have significant association on poverty.

The same exercise for landless households showed that the size of the family has a significant impact on poverty. They used the multiple regression technique to measure the influence of variables such as annual wage income, number of days employed during the year, number of workers, number of members in the family, workers as per cent of members in the household and size of land holding on per capita income. The study observed an increase in the per capita income by 0.65 as a result of an increase in employment per worker per day. An increase in the wage rate by a rupee is associated with an increase in per capita income by Rs.121.15. Thus, the authors underlined the need for employment oriented technology for ameliorating rural poverty. They used the multiple regression technique to measure the influence of variables such as annual wage income, number of days employed during the year, number of workers, number of members in the family, workers as per cent of members in the household and size of land holding on per capita income. The study observed an increase in the per capita income by 0.65 as a result of an increase in employment per worker per day. An increase in the wage rate by a rupee is associated with an increase in per capita income by Rs.121.15. Thus, the authors underlined the need for employment oriented technology for ameliorating rural poverty.

Subramanyam (1986) has identified the inter-relationships between poverty and unemployment and labour force participation rates in the East Godavari district of Andhra Pradesh (covering rural and urban segments) on the basis of the 32nd round (1977-78) of N.S.S. (state sample) data. The poverty line was by estimating the expenditure-calorie intake relationship and deriving the expenditure corresponding to the minimum calorie requirement. The calorie-expenditure relationship was given by C = f (x), where 'c' is the calorie-intake and ' x ' is the per capita total expenditure. The poverty line (x) was derived from the above relationship by inverse interpolation. The poverty lines were estimated at 3 calorie levels: 1,800, 2,000 and 2,250. In addition, Head Count Ratio and Sen's index were also used to measure the incidence of poverty. The study revealed that the incidence of poverty was not much different between rural and urban areas. However, it was higher among the scheduled castes (57.2 and 75.6 per cent in rural and urban areas respectively) than other caste people (43.2 and 47.4 per cent in rural and urban areas respectively). Classification of households by occupation groups revealed a positive association between poverty and unemployment. The incidence of poverty and unemployment being found highest among labour households with a high participation rate, the study suggested a policy of employment generation to mitigate their poverty.

The study by **Thakur (1986)** estimated the extent of rural poverty among the households belonging to Marginal Holdings, Small and Medium size in Himachal Pradesh (in the year 1980-81) on the basis of primary data. Two poverty lines were considered. They are - (i) on the basis of 'nutrition norms' (who consume less than 2,400 calories per day spent less than Rs.52.93 per month on food items), (ii) on the basis of 'nutrition plus approach' (those persons who spent less than Rs.77.61 per month on both food and non-food items). On the basis of nutritional norm approach, the percentage of poor on the marginal size of holdings was found 71.06, on the small size of holdings 50.65 and on the medium size of holdings 26.34 per cent. The overall percentage of the poor among all households was 47.14. On the basis of nutrition plus approach the percentage of poor among all the households worked out to 57.31. Here too, the percentage of poor was the highest among marginal farmers.

Radhakrishna et.al (1982) has studied the impact of liquor consumption on poverty in Ahmadabad slums for the period 1973 on the basis of primary data. The study attempted to answer the following questions, (i) what is the effect of liquor consumption on poverty? (ii) Can it make a dent on poverty if the expenditure on liquor is diverted to essential items of consumption? The study found consumption of liquor not predominantly at the cost of essential items. There was not any evidence of adverse effects of liquor consumption on the level of living. The study noticed that even if the addicts stop drinking and spend the amount on consumer items, it could not make any significant improvement on total poverty. The poverty was seen to be so deep that hardly any difference can be made to it by the diversification of the amount spent on liquor. The study highlighted the fact that the root causes of poverty lie deep in the abject conditions in which these vulnerable sections live and not in their budget allocations. It is the level of their earnings and not so much their allocation that lies at the root of rampant poverty.

Mittar's (1986) study measured the extent of poverty and the structure of income and its distribution in the informal and formal sectors in Patiala City on the basis of primary data. The author revealed that the average income of the workers in the informal sector substantially lower than that of those in the formal sector. A higher proportion of households were found lying below the poverty line in the informal sector. This was due to the low wage which was lower than the legal minimum wage. In addition, the intensity of poverty was found higher among migrant households. Further, the study also noticed a greater intensity of poverty among the nuclear family than that of a joint family.

Mitra (1987) examined the relationship between (i) landownership and poverty and (ii) size of the household and poverty in the rural area of three districts of Andhra Pradesh (Anantapur, Medak and West Godavari) during the year 1977-78. The study was on the basis of the employment-unemployment schedule of the N.S.S. (state sample) data. The dependent variables considered were monthly per capita expenditures of cultivator and agricultural labour households. The explanatory variables were: (i) the size of the household, (ii) per capita un-irrigated land, (iii) per capita irrigated land, (iv) proportion of economically active persons and (v) proportion of economically active males. The pattern of relationships between family size and the levels of living (per capita monthly expenditure) was observed to be irregular. For cultivator household's higher household size have not reduced the per capita expenditure. But the per capita expenditure of agricultural labour households was seen to be reduced by higher size of the family. Land was observed to be an important variable determining the per capita expenditure for the cultivator households. Owning and operating some land was observed to have helped in improving the per capita expenditure of the agricultural labour households. A substantial percentage of variations remained unexplained by the variables chosen for the study.

In another study **Reddy and Mitra (1982)** examined the nature of poverty and factors influencing poverty in the rural areas of Medak in Andhra Pradesh. The study relied on the ungrouped N.S.S. data of 32nd round (1977-76 state sample). The poverty line was arrived on the basis of an optimum food basket by minimizing the food cost subject to the fulfillment of nutritional norms. In their poverty line a certain imputed expenditure on non-food articles were added on the basis of the observed behaviour. They have considered a calorie requirement of 2,250 and 1,900 per capita per day. The calorie-intake of each household was derived from the information on quantities consumed by various food Items and their calorie-content. Next the per capita calorie-intake was regressed on per capita consumer expenditure using the log-log inverse form of the Engel Function:

$$\text{i.e., } \text{Log } Ci = a + b \text{ Log } Ei + c\ (l/Ei> + ei$$

Where

Ci = Per capita Calorie-intake of the ith household.

Ei = Per capita total monthly consumer expenditure of the ith household

ei = Error term.

Further, the poverty lines corresponding to calorie norms (2,250 and 1,900 calories) were derived by inverse interpolation. The study revealed that 83 and 51 per cent of the people are below the poverty line on the basis of 2,250 and 1,900 calories respectively. Among occupation groups, poverty level varied from 90 per cent for marginal farmers to 86 per cent for the landless (agricultural landless labour and the self-employed). The study observed a positive association between poverty level and average size of the household while the association was negative between poverty and the extent of irrigation. The authors suggested irrigation as an important policy instrument for the reduction of poverty and landless; marginal and small farmers to be identified as target groups for any programme of poverty eradication.

Sarma (1987) examined the 'generational' and 'temporal' dimension of poverty among agricultural labour households in the Krishna district of Andhra Pradesh (during 1981-1982) on the basis of primary data. Two poverty lines were considered. They are.- (i) An annual per capita consumption expenditure of Rs.236 at 1961-62 prices and (ii) households who own assets less than Rs.5,000.The study revealed that 41 per cent of the households were below the income poverty line, whereas it was 26 per cent in the case of landed and 47 In the case of landless households. On the basis of asset poverty, 73 per cent are below the poverty line. The relatively low incidence of poverty on the basis of Income poverty is due to the high level of development attained by the district and also due to the rise in the real wages and money wages of agricultural labour. No significant association was observed between caste and poverty. However, poverty was identified with specific occupational groups. Higher family size and dependency ratio were found to be independent factors explaining poverty. In addition, significant association between poverty and absence of female workers was also observed. However, there was not any association between poverty and the level of employment. A generational decline in occupational status and access to land were observed and this was found to have aggravated the problem of poverty. Further, inter-generational occupational change was seen more in the case of other castes that scheduled castes. The decline in the access to land among the sample households was due to the adverse effect of tenancy reforms. The regression equation estimated with per capita income as the dependent variable revealed that family size, labour force participation rate, level of employment per worker, average daily wage rate per worker and occupational holding put together have shown a high explanatory power In explaining inter-household variations In per capita Income. The author suggested public intervention in favour of the poor to make a big difference in the levels of living of the poor.

Centre of Regional Studies (1982), Utkal University, measured the extent of rural poverty in the two villages (Basantapur Sasam and Kaushalyapur) of the district of Puri in Orissa in 1982 on the basis of primary data. Poverty was measured in terms of per capita income, per capita consumption expenditure and per capita calorie-intake. On the basis of calorie-intake, the study found about 52 and 44 per cent households below the poverty line in Kaushalyapur and Basantapur villages respectively. A comparison of the incidence of poverty by calorie-intake and Per capita monthly expenditure showed higher incidence of poverty when monthly per capita expenditure criterion was used. This was on account of the fact that, in rural areas all consumption articles did not involve expenditure. The major cause of poverty was the non-availability of agricultural land to majority of the households. In addition, illiteracy, high dependency ratio, non-diversification of occupation from traditional to modern was the other factors responsible for the poverty of the region.

The study by **Thakurtha** estimated the extent of poverty in the Kolkata **(for the period 1950-72)** on the basis of the family budget enquiries undertaken by the Bureau of Applied Economics and Statistics, West Bengal. The poverty line was 2,100 calorie and it was estimated that on an average a monthly per capita income of Rs.25.89 was necessary for this much calorie in 1950-51. A per capita income of Rs.24.02, Rs.28.99, Rs.41.54 and Rs.52.57 were necessary in 1955-56, 1960-61, 1966-67 and 1971-72 respectively for generating the above mentioned calorie. The study unfolded that about 42 per cent of the people were below the poverty line in 1950-51. For the years 1955-56, 1960-61, 1966-67 and 1971-72 these percentages were 42, 44, 38 and 35 respectively. For the period under study some improvement was noticed in the economic condition of the comparatively better-off sections of the individuals living below the poverty line. Such a commensurate improvement was not seen in the lot of those living further below the poverty line. Thus, the author concluded that the rate of economic growth of the less poor in the city has been higher than that of the poorer.

CHAPTER IV

Analysis of MDGs: A Case of Poverty and Hunger in India

The Millennium Declaration, made during the UN Millennium Summit on 8 September 2000, was signed by 189 countries, including 147 Heads of State and Government, and included eight (8) Goals called the Millennium Development Goals (MDGs).They agreed to "spare no effort to free our fellow men, women and children from the abject and dehumanizing conditions of extreme poverty to which more than a billion of them are currently subjected." These summarize the key development goals embraced by the main international conferences and world summits during the 1990s, and are declarations of solidarity and determination of the world leaders to rid the world of poverty and improve the lot of humanity. MDGs and related targets and indicators provide a framework for planning policy interventions and benchmarks to monitor progress in human development and poverty reduction. Eighteen (18) targets were set as quantitative benchmarks for attaining the 8 MDGs. The United Nations Development Group (UNDG) in its 2nd Guidance note (endorsed in 2003) on 'Country

Reporting on the Millennium Development Goals' provided a framework of 53 indicators (48 basic + 5 alternative)which are categorized according to targets, for measuring the progress towards individual targets. India's MDG framework is as per the UNDG's 2003 framework for monitoring of the 8 MDGs. Out of the 18 targets, 12 targets (Target 1 to 11 and Target 18) are relevant to India.Corresponding to the 12 targets, there are 35 identified indicators.

The Millennium Declaration of 2000 consolidates and restates the commitments agreed during the preceding decade, and can be seen as the final stage of the Summit process. For the first time in a document of its kind, it stresses that, without policies and mechanisms to mobilize private and public resources on a much larger scale, the internationally agreed Millennium Development Goals (MDGs) for reducing poverty and hunger and for social and sustainable development cannot be achieved. The Declaration is thus a starting point for renewed action in the twenty-first century. The International Conference on Financing for Development can redress the failures and biases of the past by making its prime objective that of ensuring adequate funding for the achievement of the MDGs. In view of its diversity in consumption pattern and heterogeneity of market prices across the country and non-availability of an acceptable purchasing power parity index for different regions of the country, compilation/ reporting of the proportion of people whose income is less than $1 a day is not plausible in the Indian context.

Table 4.1 Millennium Development Goals Framework

MDG Goals & Target	Indicators as per UNDG frame work 2003	Indicators as per Indian frame work
Goal 1: Eradicate extreme poverty and hunger		
Target 1: Halve, between 1990 and 2015, the proportion of people whose income is less than one dollar a day		
	1. Proportion of population below$1.25 (PPP) per day	1A. Poverty Headcount Ratio
	1A. Poverty headcount ratio (percentage of population below the national poverty line)	(percentage of population below the national poverty line)
	2. Poverty gap ratio [incidence depth of poverty]	2. Poverty Gap ratio
	3. Share of poorest quintile in national consumption	3. Share of poorest quintile in national consumption

MDG Goals & Target	Indicators as per UNDG frame work 2003	Indicators as per Indian frame work
Target 2: Halve, between 1990 and 2015, the proportion of people who suffer from Hunger		
	4. Prevalence of underweight children under 5 years of age	4. Prevalence of underweight children under three years of age.
	5. Proportion of population below minimum level of dietary energy consumption	

Source : *MDG Report, Government of India(2013)*

Table 4.2 MDGs and Targets - Overview of progress achieved by India

MDG 1: Eradicate extreme poverty and hunger	
Target 1: Halve, between 1990 and 2015, the proportion of people whose income is less than one dollar a day (Percentage of Population below the National Poverty Line is considered for India for statistical tracking)	On-track
Target 2:Halve, between 1990 and 2015, the proportion of people who suffer from hunger	Slow or almost off-track

Source : *MDG Report, Government of India (2014)*

As per the poverty estimates of 2011-12, the Poverty Head Count Ratio **(PHCR)** is 21.9% thus India has already achieved the target against the target of 23.9%. With the historical rate of decline in Poverty HCR, the Country is likely to achieve PHCR level of 20.74% by 2015. Poverty Gap Ratio **(PGR)** which reflects the degree to which mean consumption of the poor falls short of the established poverty line, indicating the depth of poverty was 5.05 for Rural and 2.70 for Urban India in 2011-12. Share of Poorest Quintile in National Consumption **(MRP-Mixed Recall Period)** is 9.75 in Rural India and 7.11 in Urban India in 2009-10.All-India trend of the **proportion of underweight (severe and moderate) children below 3 years of age** shows India is going slow in eliminating the effect of malnourishment. According to the NFHS estimates, the proportion of underweight children has declined by 3 percentage points during 1998-99 to 2005-06, from about 43% to about 40%. At the historical rate of decline, **it is expected to come down to about 33% only by 2015 vis –a vis the target value of 26%.**

Estimates of Planning Commission and India's MDG Report 2014

The proportion of people below the national poverty line (poverty headcount ratio or PHCR) estimated for 1990 was 37.2%. India is required to reduce it by half to 18.6% by 2015. By the year 2004-05, the PHCR has come down to 27.5%. Going by the rate of change in the last 15 years, the projected PHCR in the year 2015 is expected to be just short of the year's MDG-target mark (18.6%) by about

3.5 percentage points. The historical rate of decline of 0.8 percent per annum in poverty ratio during 1990-2005 has shown a sign of improvement during 2005-06 as the rate of decline from the previous year's poverty ratio is estimated to be 1.4 percent. Even at the historical pace (at the rate of decline during 1990-2005), as many as 21 States/UTs are likely to halve their 1990 levels of the poverty ratio earlier than 2015 and 4 more States are on track to achieving the targets of halving their 1990 poverty ratios by 2015. The absolute number of poor in the country has declined from about 320 million (36% of total population) in 1993-94 to about 301 million (27.6% of total population) in 2004-05. At this rate of decline, the country is expected to have a burden of about 279 million of people (22.1%) living below the poverty line in the year 2015. The major States namely, Bihar, Jharkhand, Chhattisgarh, Madhya Pradesh, Maharashtra, Orissa, Uttar Pradesh and Uttarakhand, which are incidentally the more populated States, are among the slow-moving States in reducing the poverty and are not likely to achieve their target of halving the poverty ratio of 1990 by 2015 going at the pace they moved during 1990-2005. These States had about 193.5 million of people below poverty line in 2004-05 (64% of total BPL 2 population) and are expected to have nearly 198 million people below poverty line in 2015 (71% of total projected BPL population). The contours of socio-economic development in these heartland States of India will continue to remain in focus. Let's analyze the estimates of poverty by planning commission and can have a brief scanning of Millennium Development Goals as follows:

MDG 1: Eradicate extreme poverty and hunger

Target 1 Halve, between 1990 and 2015, the proportion of people whose income is less than one dollar a day

Indicators

- Poverty Headcount Ratio (percentage of population below the national poverty line)
- Poverty Gap ratio
- Share of poorest quintile in national consumption

Target 2 Halve, between 1990 and 2015, the proportion of people who suffer from hunger

Indicator

- Prevalence of underweight children under three years of age.

Source : GoI: Planning Commission, New Delhi

- Poverty Head Count Ratio {(PHCR) percentage of population below the national poverty line}

India, the world's second most populous country is home to 1.2 billion people, which is 17 percent of the world population. In this country of huge diversities, poverty has always been a cause of great concern always. However, as the statistics reveals, over the years, India has made significant progress in poverty reduction. The official poverty estimates released by Planning Commission (Tendulkar methodology) based on NSSO Survey on Household Consumer Expenditure

2011-12 reveal that, the all-India Poverty Head Count Ratio (PHCR) has declined by 15 percentage points from 37.2 percent in 2004-05 to 21.9 percent in 2011-12. Significant decline in poverty ratio has been observed in both rural and urban areas during this period as the rural poverty head count ratio declined by 16 percentage points from 41.8 percent to 25.7 percent and urban poverty declining by 12 percentage points from 25.7 percent to 13.7 percent. Though, the nation shows considerable improvement in poverty reduction, it is alarming that, still, 1 in every 5persons in India is below the national poverty line.

While considering the progress towards MDG target 1, the estimate of PHCR at the national level was at 47.8 percent for 1990 and the Country is required to achieve a PHCR level of 23.9 percent by 2015 in order to meet the MDG target. With a faster decline in PHCR i.e. annual decline of 1.9 percentage points during 2004-12,compared to 0.7 percentage points during 1993-2004, the country has already achieved the MDG target, which is a notable achievement.

Source: *GoI: Planning Commission, New Delhi*

Figure 4.1 Poverty Headcount Ratio

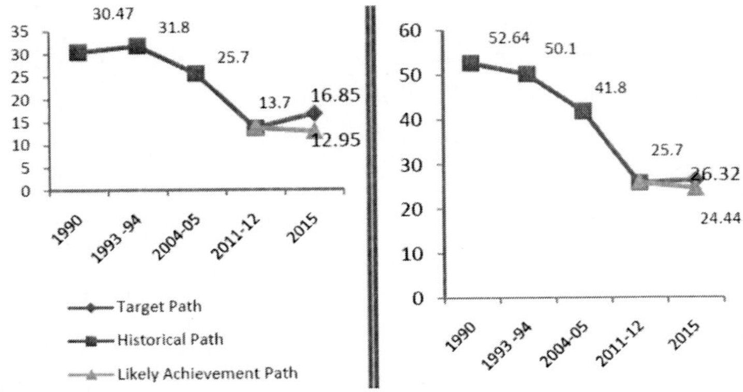

Source: *GoI: Planning Commission, New Delhi*

Figure 4.2 Trends in Poverty Head Count ratio- Rural and Urban India

As per Census 2011, in India, 69 percent of its population is in rural areas, and thus majority of the poor people belongs to rural India. The Census 2011 Population results and the latest poverty head count ratio (2011-12) points out that, out of the 270 million poor people of India, 81 percent (217 millions) are from rural India. The trend of decline in poverty ratio is evident in both rural and urban areas and the decline was from PHCR from 25.7 in 2004-05 to 13.7 in 2011-12 in urban areas and from 41.8 to 25.7 in rural areas. With the recent sharper decline in PHCR, the MDG target has already been achieved in both rural and urban areas. The Rural –Urban gap in poverty ratio has come down from 18 percentage points in1993-94 to 12 percentage points, in 2011-12 and this persisting wide gap in Rural Urban Poverty Ratio is a cause of concern. In all States, except Punjab (Rural: 7.66, Urban: 9.24), rural poverty ratio was higher and the rural – urban gap in PHCR varied from 1 percentage point (Uttar Pradesh - Rural: 11.62, Urban: 10.48) to 29 percentage points (Mizoram Rural: 35.43, Urban: 6.36).

Table 4.3 Poverty Head Count Ratio (PHCR) – States arranged in the ascending order of PHCR

Rank	State	PHCR 2011-12	State	PHCR 2004-05
1	Goa	5.09	Nagaland	9
2	Kerala	7.05	Delhi	13.1
3	Himachal Pradesh	8.06	Jammu Kashmir	13.2
4	Sikkim	8.19	Pondicherry	14.1
5	Punjab	8.26	Mizoram	15.3
6	Andhra Pradesh	9.2	Meghalaya	16.1
7	Pondicherry	9.69	Kerala	19.7

Rank	State	PHCR 2011-12	State	PHCR 2004-05
8	Delhi	9.91	Punjab	20.9
9	Jammu Kashmir	10.35	Himachal Pradesh	22.9
10	Haryana	11.16	Haryana	24.1
11	Uttarakhand	11.26	Goa	25
12	Tamil Nadu	11.28	Tamil Nadu	28.9
13	Meghalaya	11.87	Andhra Pradesh	29.9
14	Tripura	14.05	Arunachal Pradesh	31.1
15	Rajasthan	14.71	Sikkim	31.1
16	Gujarat	16.63	Gujarat	31.8

Rank	State	PHCR 2011-12	State	PHCR 2004-05
17	Maharashtra	17.35	Uttarakhand	32.7
18	Nagaland	18.88	Karnataka	33.4
19	West Bengal	19.98	West Bengal	34.3
20	Mizoram	20.4	Assam	34.4
21	Karnataka	20.91	Rajasthan	34.4
22	Uttar Pradesh	29.43	Manipur	38
23	Madhya Pradesh	31.65	Maharashtra	38.1
24	Assam	31.98	Tripura	40.6
25	Odisha	32.59	Uttar Pradesh	40.9

Rank	State	PHCR 2011-12	State	PHCR 2004-05
26	Bihar	33.74	Jharkhand	45.3
27	Arunachal Pradesh	34.67	Madhya Pradesh	48.6
28	Manipur	36.89	Chattisgarh	49.4
29	Jharkhand	36.96	Bihar	54.4
30	Chattisgarh	39.93	Odisha	57.2
	All India	**21.9**	**All India**	**37.2**

Source : *GoI: Planning Commission, New Delhi*

As per the PHCR estimates of 2011-12, the lowest PHCR is for the State of Goa (5.09 percent) followed by Kerala (7.05percent). The highest PHCR is for the State of Chattisgarh (39.93 percent) followed by Jharkhand (36.96 percent) and Manipur (36.89 percent). The poverty ratios of 2004-05 and 2011-12, in the ascending order of PHCR are given at table 4.3.

The State/ UT wise results of poverty head count ratio reflects the extent of poverty in State/ UTs and the progress over the years in reducing poverty. During 2011-12, the Poverty ratio in Uttarakhand, Tripura, Sikkim, Maharashtra, and Bihar, has declined by about 20 percentage points or more in comparison to 2004-05. In Arunachal Pradesh, Mizoram and Nagaland, PHCR has increased during 2004-12.During this period, the States of Goa, Sikkim, Uttarakhand, Andhra Pradesh, Tripura, Himachal Pradesh, Kerala, Tamil Nadu, Punjab, Rajasthan, Maharashtra and Haryana recorded more than 50 percent reduction in PHCR.

Performance of States in Achieving MDG Target

In 2011-12, the States of Uttar Pradesh, Madhya Pradesh, Assam, Odisha, Bihar, Arunachal Pradesh, Manipur, Jharkhand and Chhattisgarh have PHCR above the national level estimate (21.9 percent) and the remaining 21 States have PHCR below the national level estimate. All States, except Assam, Arunachal Pradesh, Uttar Pradesh, Manipur, Madhya Pradesh, Odisha, Bihar, Jharkhand and

Chhattisgarh are likely to achieve the national level MDG target by 2015. The performance of States vis-a-vis, their respective MDG target is significant to assess the progress with respect to the respective MDG base year i.e., 1990. As per the historical trend, 23 States are likely to achieve their respective MDG target by 2015. Delhi, Bihar, Uttar Pradesh and Odisha are likely to miss their MDG target narrowly, and the States of Madhya Pradesh, Chattisgarh and Mizoram are likely to miss their MDG targets by huge margin.

Indicator: Poverty Gap Ratio (PGR)

Improve the lot of the poorest of the poor, is equally important as reducing the quantum of poverty. The indicator of Poverty Gap Ratio (PGR) reflects the degree to which mean consumption of the poor falls short of the established poverty line, indicating the depth of poverty. During 2004-05 to 2011-12, the Poverty Gap Ratio (estimated from monthly per capita consumption expenditure data based on Mixed Recall Period (MRP)) has shown decline in rural and urban areas. In rural areas, PGR declined from 9.22 in 2004-05 to 5.05 in 2011-12, while in urban areas the decline was from 6.08 to 2.7 during this period. Poverty Gap Ratio helps to provide an overall assessment of a region's progress in poverty alleviation and the evaluation of specific public policies or private initiatives. The State wise trend in PGR in rural areas (in ascending order of PGR in 2011-12) is depicted in **Figure 4.3** In 2011-12, Poverty Gap Ratio in rural areas was above the corresponding all India figure in the States of Uttar Pradesh, Assam, Bihar, Manipur, Jharkhand, Odisha,

Mizoram, Madhya Pradesh, Chattisgarh and Arunachal Pradesh. The States of Nagaland, Mizoram, Meghalaya, Manipur, and Arunachal Pradesh had shown increase in PGR in rural areas during 2004-05 to 2011-12, whereas other States showed decline in PGR during this period, and considerable decline was observed in the States of Odisha, Tripura, Maharashtra, Bihar and Gujarat

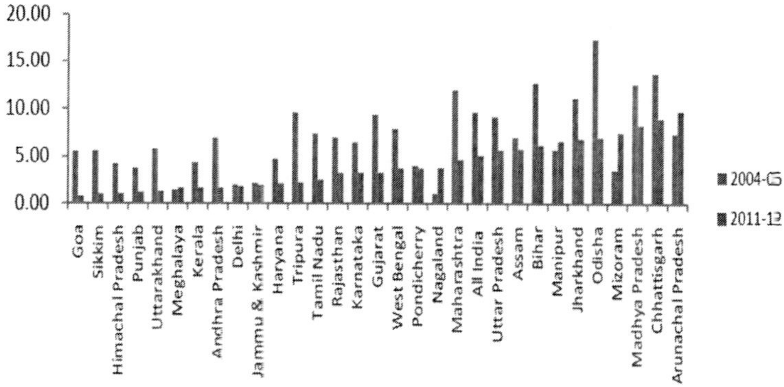

Source: *GoI: Planning Commission, New Delhi*

Figure 4.3 Trend in Poverty Gap Ratio (PGR) –Rural India

The State wise trend in PGR in Urban areas (in ascending order of PGR in 2011-12) is depicted in Fig 3.6. In 2011-12, the States of Karnataka, Odisha, Assam, Madhya Pradesh, Jharkhand, Arunachal Pradesh, Chattisgarh, Uttar Pradesh, Manipur and Bihar have PGR in urban areas above the corresponding national level estimate. During 2004-05 to 2011-12, PGR in urban areas has increased in Nagaland, Arunachal Pradesh and Manipur, whereas the remaining States showed reduction.

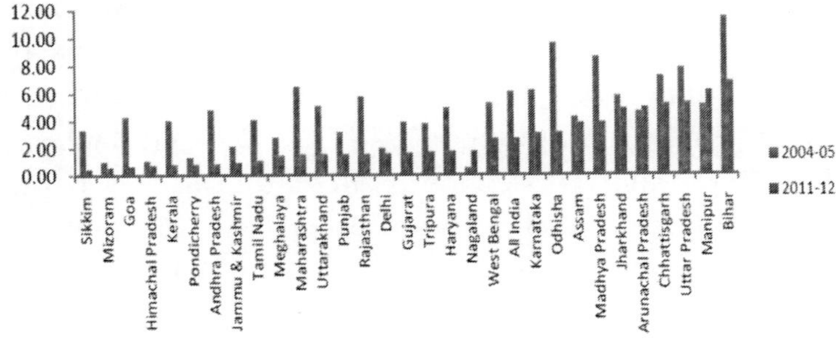

Source: *GoI: Planning Commission, New Delhi*

Figure 4.4 Trend in Poverty Gap Ratio (PGR) – Urban India

The recent trend of increase in poverty head count ratio as well as poverty gap ratio in some States i.e. Arunachal Pradesh, Mizoram and Nagaland is quite worrying, indicating urgent need for more intensive and effective measures of poverty alleviation.

Indicator: Share of Poorest Quintile in National Consumption

The share of the poorest 20 percent population in terms of the monthly per capita consumption expenditure in total consumption (i.e. consumption accounted for by the poorest one fifth of the population) in the rural areas declined from 9.6 percent in 1993-94 to 9.5 percent in 2004-05 based on (Uniform Reference Period – URP method) and NSS 2009-10 (Modified Reference period – MRP method) reported a slightly increased level i.e. 9.8 percent. In the urban areas the share of the poorest 20 percent population, declined from 8 percent in 1993-94 to 7.3 percent in 2004-05 and to 7.1 percent in

2009-10. This decrease in the share of consumption expenditure for the poorest quintile is indicative of growing inequities, particularly in the urban areas.

The persisting low levels of anthropometric indicators of nutrition in India, for both adults and children even in the midst of intensified initiatives for poverty alleviation, is a cause of great concern. Intake of dietary energy per person continues to be the most widely used indicator of the level of nutrition of a population.

Table 4.4 Share of poorest quintile in national consumption

	1993-94 (URP)	2004-2005 (URP)	2009-10 (MRP)
Rural	9.6	9.5	9.8
Urban	8.0	7.3	7.1

Source: *NSS report 538, Level and Pattern of Consumer Expenditure*

The NSSO surveys held during 1993-2010, to study nutritional intake in India, revealed that, estimated per capita calorie intake was more in rural areas than urban areas in all the rounds, except 1999-2000, in which the estimated per capita calorie intake for urban areas was slightly more than rural areas. In both urban and rural areas, declining trend has been observed in the estimated per capita calorie intake per day during this period and there was nearly 6 percent decline in 2009-10 in both rural and urban areas compared to 1993-94.

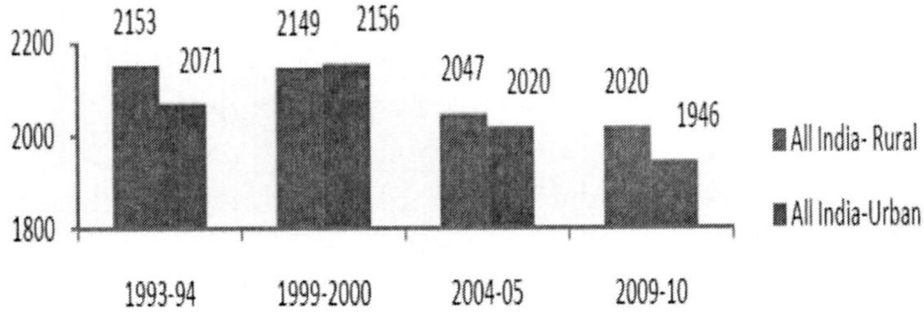

Source: *GoI: Planning Commission, New Delhi*

Figure 4.5 Trend in estimated per capita calorie intake-All India

Further, the trend of decline in per capita calorie intake per day during 2004-05 to 2009-10, reveals that, though the decline was reported both in rural and urban areas, the extent of decline was more in urban areas. Among the major States, estimated per capita calorie intake (Kcal) per day in rural areas was highest in Punjab (2223 Kcal) and lowest in Jharkhand (1900 Kcal) in 2009-10 and in urban areas, the highest per capita calorie intake (Kcal) per day was reported in Odisha (2096 Kcal) and lowest in West Bengal (1851 Kcal). During 2004-05 to 2009-10, in rural areas, 8 major States i.e. Andhra Pradesh, Gujarat, Karnataka, Maharashtra, Orissa, Rajasthan, Tamil Nadu and Uttarakhand, reported a rise in estimated per capita calorie intake per day, while, the remaining major States reported a decline. In the Urban areas, only three major States i.e. Karnataka, Maharashtra and Tamil Nadu reported a rise in estimated per capita calorie intake (Kcal) per day during this period, while the rest of the major States reported decline. The decline in per capita calorie intake per day in most of the States in spite of the economic development and ongoing initiatives towards poverty alleviation is a matter of concern.

Indicator: Prevalence of underweight children under three years of age

Children are the worst sufferers of poverty and malnourishment among children are a significant indicator of food insecurity. The indicator '**Prevalence of underweight children**' is the percentage of children under three years of age whose weight for age is less than minus two standard deviations from the median for the reference population aged 0-35 months5. All-India trend of the **proportion of underweight (severe and moderate) children below 3 years of age** 6 shows India is showing a slow progress in eliminating the effect of malnourishment. From estimated 52 per cent in 1990, the proportion of underweight children below 3 years is required to be reduced to 26 per cent by 2015. The proportion of underweight children has declined by 3 percentage points during 1998-99 **(NFHS -2)** to 2005-06 **(NFHS-3)**, from about 43 per cent to about 40 per cent and at this historical rate of decline, it is expected to come down to about 33 per cent only by 2015. As per NFHS -3, in India, one in every three children in the age group of 0-3 years is suffering from under weight. Census 2011, reports nearly 89 million children in the age group 0-3 years and with the 40 per cent prevalence of underweight, 35.6 million among them are underweight children. The indicator of underweight (weight-for-age - inadequate weight-for-age indicate underweight), together with the indicator of stunting (height-for-age - inadequate height-for-age indicate stunting) and wasting (weight-for-height - inadequate weight-for-height indicate wasting) reveals a better picture of nutritional status of children.

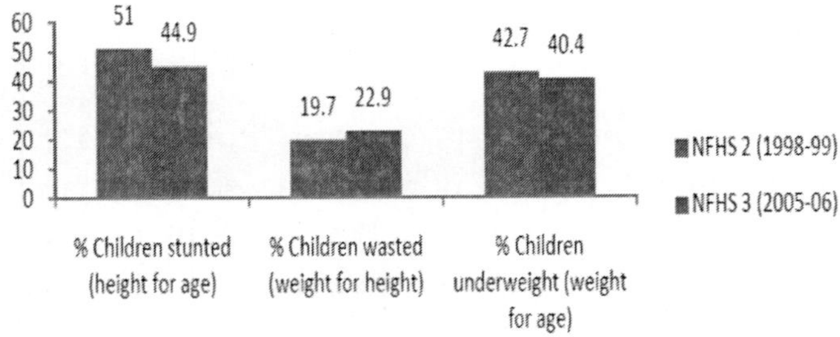

Source: *GoI: Planning Commission, New Delhi*

Figure 4.6 Nutritional Status of Children under three years of age in India

During the period between NFHS 2 (1998-99) & NFHS 3 (2005-06), decline has been observed for prevalence of stunting and underweight among children under 3 years of age, whereas the percentage of children 'wasted' has increased. However, it may be noted that, the degree of decline was very low for both the cases of stunting and underweight children (< 3 years) as the per year decline were less than one percentage point in both cases. Further, the increase in the 'percentage of children wasted' over years indicates a worsening situation, though per year increase was less than one percentage point.

Underweight children <3 years – Profile of States/ UTs

Nutritional problems are substantial in every State in India. The proportion of children under age five years who are underweight was lowest in Mizoram (14.2 per cent) followed by Sikkim (17.3 per cent). The States which are above the national level estimate (40 per cent) of children under three years of age underweight are Gujarat (41.1 per cent), Uttar Pradesh (41.6 per cent), Meghalaya (42.9 per cent), Chattisgarh (47.8 per cent), Jharkhand (54.6 per cent), Bihar (54.9 per cent) and Madhya Pradesh (57.9 per cent).

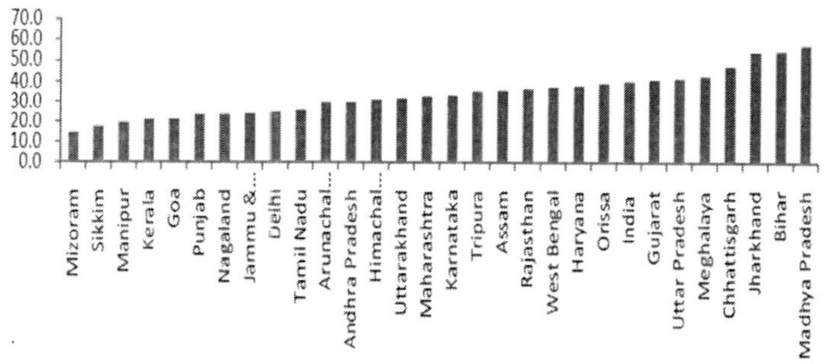

Source: GoI: Planning Commission, New Delhi

Figure 4.7 Prevalence of underweight children under three years of age (2005-06)

As per NFHS -3 results, 10 States namely Mizoram (14.2 per cent), Sikkim (17.3 per cent), Manipur (19.5 per cent), Kerala (21.2 per cent), Goa (21.3 per cent), Punjab (23.6 per cent), Nagaland (23.7 per cent), Jammu & Kashmir (24 per cent), Delhi (24.9 per cent), and Tamil Nadu (25.9 per cent)have already achieved the all India MDG target for prevalence of underweight children under three years of age and four more States i.e. Andhra Pradesh, Karnataka, Maharashtra and Uttarakhand are likely to achieve the target by 2015. However, as per the historical trend, only 6 States, namely, Maharashtra,

Andhra Pradesh, Tamil Nadu, Delhi, Jammu & Kashmir and Punjab are likely to achieve their own MDG targets by 2015.

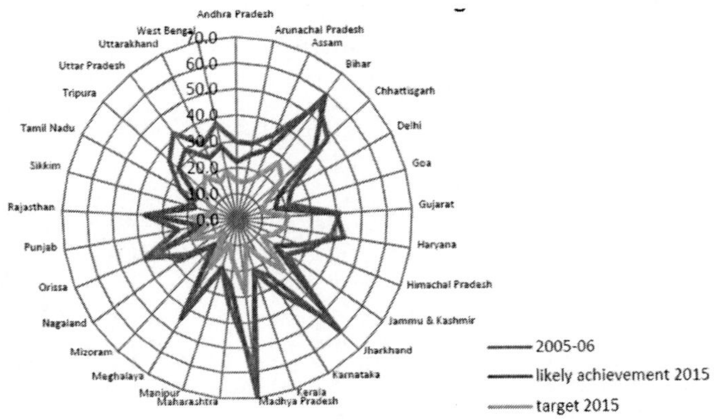

Source: *GoI: Planning Commission, New Delhi*

Figure 4.8 Prevalence of underweight children < three years likely achievements of states vis-à-vis MDG Target 2015

The statistics as discussed above, points out that, majority of the States are crippled with the problem of malnutrition and the issue invites special attention in the context of declining trend observed in per capita nutritional intake. The gap existing in the present nutritional status among children (measured by prevalence of underweight children) from the MDG target and the declining trend in the estimate per capita nutritional intake per day in majority of the States indicates the complexity of the issue of malnutrition and hunger.

Where India Stands and Struggles?

Planning commission defines poverty line on the basis of Monthly Per Capita Expenditure(MPCE).Prof. Suresh D. Tendulkar report (2009) has computed the poverty lines at all India levels as MPCE of Rs.447 for rural areas and Rs.579 for urban areas in 2004-05. The Planning Commission has updated the poverty lines and it has estimated the poverty lines at all India level based on MPCE of Rs. 673 for rural areas and Rs.860 for urban areas in 2009-10.Based on this, the percentage of people below poverty line has declined from 37.2 per cent to 29.8 per cent from 2004-05 to 2009-10 respectively. Thus poverty has declined on an average by 1.5 percentage points per year between 2004-5 and 2009-10. The annual average rate of decline during the period 2004-05 to 2009-10 is twice the rate of decline during the period 1993-94 to 2004-05 (Table1). The Planning Commission has also constituted an Expert Group under the Chairmanship of Dr. C. Rangarajan to 'Review the Methodology for Measurement of Poverty' in June 2012 and he examined and made an interstate comparison in terms of several socio-economic indicators. We can have a quick scanning about index of poverty based on interstate comparison

Table 4.5 Number of Percentage of Poor

Year	Number of poor(Million)			Poverty Ratio (per cent)		
	Rural	Urban	Total	Rural	Urban	Total
1993-94	328.6	74.5	403.7	50.1	31.8	45.3
2004-05	326.3	80.8	407.1	41.8	25.07	37.2
2009-10	278.2	76.5	354.7	33.8	20.9	29.8
Annual average decline (1993-94 to 2004-05)				0.75	0.55	0.74
Annual average decline (2004-05 to 2009-10)				1.60	0.96	1.48

Source: *GoI: Planning Commission, New Delhi, Estimated by Tendulkar Method.*

But India struggles somewhere which is mainly on the part of bureaucratic policy makers who involved in estimation of poverty. They probably failed in channelising the fruits of mixed strategies, policies and programmes of the governments, meant for poor and weaker sections. The results arrived from the data support evident from the writings of Himanshu et al (2010) postulated and brought out few reasons and provided a new message that seems to be significant in redefining poverty lines. Economists may have differences in poverty estimation methodology and thus their estimates may vary in magnitude. But two things we can surely say from the Minhas estimation of poverty and Current estimation methods followed by the recommendations of Tendulkar. The first thing is that The percentage of population below poverty line started declining as a result of indirect benefits of higher growth rate and also the impact of different poverty alleviation in rural development programmes. But still 37 per cent remains to be below poverty line. Secondly, the absolute number of poor has certainly increased over the years.

Thomas Pogge, Mitu Sengupta reveal their anxious through their work "New Millennium Development Goals; A New Version, an Old Wish List" that high-level United Nations panel has proposed the adoption of 12 new Millennium Development Goals from 2015. The new goals suffer from the same key defects as the original ones; they are general wishes without concrete tasks and responsibilities assigned to specific competent actors, and they do not meet civil society aspirations for inequality reduction, systemic reforms of global institutions, and a more comprehensive view of poverty. While the MDGs commendably bring focus on poverty and poor people, they are goals without commitments. They do while the MDGs commendably bring focus on poverty and poor people; they are goals without any major commitments. One of the poorest countries might be blamed for not reducing its hunger rate from 60 per cent to 30 per cent, while an upper middle-income country might rest easy with the much less demanding task of reducing its hunger rate from 2 per cent to 1 per cent. This is precisely what happened with the MDGs, where the poorest countries ended up being held solely responsible for not bringing down their huge deprivation rates fast enough.

The definitions and methods involved in development targets must not be allowed to be changed midway and the tracking of progress must not be entrusted to the agencies like the FAO and the World Bank, but should be left to an independent international group of top-level academic experts. Many of the hardships that constitute poverty in the real world are in different forms such as the lack of safe water, of basic education, of leisure time and of access to public officials; the scourges of debt bondage, child labour, and discrimination against women and girls which are completely ignored when one merely ascertains whether a household's income or expenditure has as much purchasing power per person per day as US$1.25 had in the US in 2005.In the context a paper by Himanshu et.al (2010) forward some suggestions for redefine research methodology for estimation of poverty which might be some of the strategically problems India facing while estimation. They are pointed as follows:

- To clarify that poverty in India is measured purely on the consumption dimension and that all other dimensions, including calorie norms on which present poverty lines were originally constructed, are incidental and only of historical significance.
- To suggest that once consumption cut-off is chosen it should apply equally
- and without discrimination to all locations, rural and urban, with the only location-specific adjustment being for differences in cost of living.
- To maintain minimum standard of living to avoid absolute poverty, there are two possible references (Mixed Reference Period & Uniform Reference Period), the present all-India urban and rural poverty lines, of which only one can be chosen since the other must be determined by actual cost of living differences.
- Official rural poverty estimates are widely perceived to be too low and no longer conforming to acceptable basic needs. Since official urban poverty estimates are less controversial, our choice of reference consumption cut-off is the MRP
- (Mixed Reference Period) equivalent of the present official all-India urban poverty line, which leaves measured all-India urban poverty incidence unchanged from its current official estimate.
- By Using MRP instead of Uniform reference Period gives the same urban poverty rate as official, rather than taking the present official urban poverty line directly, is

because the National Sample Survey (NSS) now uses the MRP rather than URP in most of its surveys. It is necessary to have poverty lines that correspond to MRP distributions.

- The new poverty lines are not based on any particular norm of basic needs, and are outcome of a purely technical exercise to calculate cost of living indices relevant around the present all-India urban poverty line, this choice can be defended normatively. In particular, albeit modest norms of nutrition and of paid-out education and health costs are adequately met at the all-India level and in most, although not all, states.

Committed towards Combating Poverty and Hunger

Poverty is a complex and multidimensional phenomenon. The institutions addressing the issues of poor therefore need to engage in many sectors and with several service providers. The Government of India has taken a number of initiatives towards eradicating poverty and hunger as poverty remains to be the major hurdle towards sustainable development in the Country.

National Food Security Mission (NFSM)

The National Development Council **(NDC)** in its 53rd meeting held on 29th May, 2007 adopted a resolution to launch Food Security Mission comprising rice, wheat and pulses to increase the production of rice by

10 million tons, wheat by 8 million tons and pulses by 2 million tons by the end of the Eleventh Plan (2011-12). Accordingly, A Centrally Sponsored Scheme, 'National Food Security Mission', has been launched from 2007-08 to operationalise the above mentioned resolution. The National Food Security Mission has 3 components (i) Rice (ii) Wheat & (iii) Pulses. The NFSM objectives are increasing production of rice, wheat and pulses through area expansion and productivity enhancement in a sustainable manner in the identified districts of the country, restoring soil fertility and productivity at the individual farm level, creation of employment opportunities, and enhancing farm level economy (i.e. farm profits) to restore confidence amongst the farmers. Under NFSM, financial support will be available for research in the following areas:

- Conservation of natural resources (land, water) and their efficient use.
- Integrated nutrient management.
- Integrated disease and pest management.
- Integrated weed management.
- Modification/refinements of farm machines/ implements for different types of soil/cropping systems.
- Up-scaling of improved crop varieties/hybrids in NFSM adopted states/agro-climatic zones under water/thermal stress conditions.
- Nutrient management in acidic/ alkaline/ sodic soils.
- Crop-husbandry.

- Input use efficiency.
- Rain-water harvesting management in kharif pulses.
- Refinement of relay cropping systems.
- Agronomic practices for intercropping systems involving pulses.
- Quality seed storage studies in the humid and hot climatic conditions-coastal areas.
- Value addition in case of coarse cereals and pulses
- Precision farming-nutrient manager and crop manager
- Any other relevant areas related to crop production

Rashtriya Krishi Vikas Yojana (RKVY)

The RKVY had aimed at achieving 4% annual growth in the agriculture sector during the XI Plan period, and is continuing in the 12th Plan, by ensuring a holistic development of Agriculture and allied sectors. The main objectives of the scheme are:

- To incentivize the states so as to increase public investment in Agriculture and allied sectors.
- To provide flexibility and autonomy to states in the process of planning and executing Agriculture and allied sector schemes.
- To ensure the preparation of agriculture plans for the districts and the states based on agro-climatic conditions, availability of technology and natural resources.

- To ensure that the local needs/crops/priorities are better reflected in the agricultural plans of the states.
- To achieve the goal of reducing the yield gaps in important crops, through focused interventions.
- To maximize returns to the farmers in agriculture and allied sectors.
- To bring about quantifiable changes in the production and productivity of various components of Agriculture and allied sectors by addressing them in a holistic manner.

Mahatma Gandhi National Rural Employment Scheme (MGNREGA)

The Mahatma Gandhi National Rural Employment Guarantee Act **(MGNREGA)** was enacted on 5th September, 2005 and came into force w.e.f. 2nd February, 2006. On 31st December, 2009, the Act was renamed by an Amendment as the Mahatma Gandhi National Rural Employment Guarantee Act, 2005. The mandate of the Act is to provide at least 100 days of guaranteed wage employment in a financial year to every rural household whose adult members volunteer to do unskilled manual work. It is provided in the Act that, while providing employment, priority shall be given to women in such a way that, at least 1/3rd of the beneficiaries shall be women, who have registered and requested for work under the Scheme. The Goals of MGNREGA are,

- Social protection for the most vulnerable people living in rural India by providing employment opportunities
- Livelihood security for the poor through creation of durable assets, improved water security, soil conservation and higher land productivity
- Drought-proofing and flood management in rural India
- Empowerment of the socially disadvantaged, especially women, Scheduled Castes (SCs) and Schedules Tribes (STs), through the processes of rights based legislation
- Strengthening decentralized, participatory planning through convergence of various anti-poverty and livelihoods initiatives
- Deepening democracy at the grass-roots by strengthening Panchayati-Raj Institutions
- Effecting greater transparency and accountability in governanceThus, MGNREGA is a powerful instrument for ensuring inclusive growth in rural India through its impact on social protection, livelihood security and democratic empowerment.

Indira Awas Yojana (IAY)

Rural housing development has to be seen in the context of poverty alleviation and overall rural development. Housing lays foundation for living with dignity for the rural poor by dispelling the gloom of being shelter-less. Indira Awas Yojana (IAY) is a centrally sponsored scheme for rural BPL families who are either houseless or having inadequate housing facilities for constructing a safe and durable shelter. IAY has the following components:

- Assistance for construction of a new house
- Upgradation of kutcha or dilapidated houses
- Provision of house sites

95 per cent of the total budget would be utilized for the components relating to new houses, upgradation of houses and provision of house sites and administrative expenses. The remaining 5 per cent would be reserved for special projects of

- Rehabilitation of BPL families affected by natural calamities
- Rehabilitation of BPL families affected by violence and law and order problems
- Settlement of freed bonded labourers and liberated manual scavengers
- Settlement of particularly vulnerable tribal groups
- New technology demonstration – especially with focus on affordable and green technologies.

National Rural Livelihood Mission (NRLM)

The Ministry of Rural Development has re-designed and re-structured the Swarnjayanti Gram Swarojgar Yojana (SGSY) into National Livelihood Mission (NRLM) as a cornerstone of national poverty reduction strategy. The objective of the Mission is to reduce poverty among rural

BPL by promoting diversified and gainful self-employment and wage employment opportunities which would lead to an appreciable increase in income on sustainable basis. In the long run, it will ensure broad based inclusive growth and reduce disparities by spreading out the benefits from the islands of growth across the regions, sectors and communities. The core belief of National Rural Livelihoods Mission (NRLM) is that the poor have innate capabilities and a strong desire to come out of poverty. They are entrepreneurial, an essential coping mechanism to survive under conditions of poverty. The challenge is to unleash their capabilities to generate meaningful livelihoods and enable them to come out of poverty. The first step in this process is motivating them to form their own institutions. They and their institutions need to be provided sufficient capacities to access finance and to expand their skills and assets and convert them into meaningful livelihoods. This requires continuous handholding support. An external dedicated, sensitive support structure, from the national level to the sub-district level, is required to induce such social mobilization, institution building and livelihoods promotion. NRLM implementation is in a Mission Mode. This enables: (a) shift from the present allocation based strategy to a demand driven strategy, enabling the States to formulate their own livelihoods-based poverty reduction action plans, (b) focus on targets, outcomes and time bound delivery, (c) continuous capacity building, imparting requisite skills and creating linkages with livelihoods opportunities for the poor, including those emerging in the organized sector, and (d) monitoring against targets of poverty outcomes. As NRLM follows a demand driven strategy, the States have the flexibility to develop their livelihoods-based perspective plans and annual action plans for poverty reduction. The second dimension of demand driven strategy implies that the ultimate objective is that the poor will drive the agenda, through participatory planning at grassroots level, implementation of their own plans, reviewing and generating further plans based on their experiences.

National Urban livelihood Mission (NULM)

The National Urban livelihood Mission (NULM) implemented by the Ministry of Housing and Urban Poverty Alleviation aims to reduce poverty and vulnerability of the urban poor households by enabling them to access gainful self employment and skilled wage employment opportunities, resulting in an appreciable improvement in their livelihoods on a sustainable basis, through building strong grassroots level institutions of the poor. The mission would aim at providing shelters equipped with essential services to the urban homeless in a phased manner. In addition, the mission would also address livelihood concerns of the urban street vendors by facilitating access to suitable spaces, institutional credit, social security and skills to the urban street vendors for accessing emerging market opportunities. The strategy followed in NULM includes,

- Building capacity of the urban poor, their institutions and the machinery involved in the implementation of livelihoods development and poverty alleviation programmes through handholding support;

- Enhancing and expanding existing livelihoods options of the urban poor;
- Building skills to enable access to growing market-based job opportunities offered by emerging urban economies;
- Training for and support to the establishment of micro-enterprises by the urban poor – self and group;
- Ensure availability and access for the urban homeless population to permanent 24-hour shelters including the basic infrastructural facilities like water supply, sanitation, safety and security;
- Cater to the needs of especially vulnerable segments of the urban homeless like the dependent children, aged, disabled, mentally ill, and recovering patients etc., by creating special sections within homeless shelters and provisioning special service linkages for them;
- To establish strong rights-based linkages with other programmes which cover the right of the urban homeless to food, healthcare, education, etc. and ensure access for homeless populations to various entitlements, including to social security pensions, PDS, ICDS, feeding programmes, drinking water, sanitation, identity, financial inclusion, school admission etc., and to affordable housing;
- To address livelihood concerns of the urban street vendors by facilitating access to suitable spaces, institutional credit, social security and skills to the urban street vendors for accessing emerging market opportunities.

Rajiv Awas Yojana (RAY)

The Rajiv Awas Yojana envisages a "Slum Free India" with inclusive and equitable cities in which every citizen has access to basic civic infrastructure, social amenities and decent shelter. The objectives of the programme are,

- Improving and provisioning of housing, basic civic infrastructure and social amenities in intervened slums.
- Enabling reforms to address some of the causes leading to creation of slums.
- Facilitating a supportive environment for expanding institutional credit linkages for the urban poor.
- Institutionalizing mechanisms for prevention of slums including creation of affordable housing stock.
- Strengthening institutional and human resource capacities at the Municipal, City and State levels through comprehensive capacity building and strengthening of resource networks.
- Empowering community by ensuring their participation at every stage of decision making through strengthening and nurturing Slum Dwellers' Association/Federation.

Integrated Child Development Services (ICDS) Scheme

The Integrated Child Development Services (ICDS) Scheme, implemented by the Ministry of Women and Child Development is an important programme of the Government and is being strengthened through various five year plans. ICDS targets fighting malnutrition among children below 6 years of age and pregnant women & lactating mothers. ICDS is a centrally sponsored Scheme being implemented by the State Governments/UT Administrations. The scheme aims at holistic development of children below 6 years of age and pregnant women & lactating mothers by providing a package of six services comprising (i) Supplementary nutrition (ii) Pre-school non34 formal education (iii) Nutrition and health Education (iv) Immunization (v) Health check-up and (vi) Referral services through Anganwadi Centres at grassroots level. The Scheme is universal and applicable to all the beneficiaries irrespective of any economic or other criteria. The key features of Strengthened and Restructured ICDS in 12th five year Plan interalia include addressing the gaps and challenges with

- Special focus on children under 3 years and pregnant and lactating mothers.
- Strengthening and repackaging of services including, care and nutrition counseling services and care of severely underweight children.
- A provision for an additional Anganwadi Worker cum Nutrition Counselor for focus on children under 3 years of age and to improve the family contact, care and nutrition counseling for P&L Mothers in the selected 200 high-burden districts across the country, besides having provision of link worker, 5 per cent creche cum Anganwadi centre.

- Focus on Early Childhood Care and Education (ECCE)
- Forging strong institutional and programmatic convergence particularly, at the district, block and village levels, improving Supplementary Nutrition Programme including cost revision among other components.

The Goals and Targets of Restructured and Strengthened ICDS are

- To prevent and reduce young child under nutrition by 10 per cent points in 0-3 years and enhance early development and learning outcomes in all children below six years of age
- Improved care and nutrition of girls and women and reduce anaemia prevalence in young children, girls and women by 1/5th and
- Achieve time bound goals and outcomes with results based monitoring of indicators at different levels.

A number of similar Programmes are being implemented by Central as well as State Governments to tackle the burden of poverty and hunger in this Country. The focused efforts to improve the lives of poor in all fronts need to be continued in a sustainable manner so as to overcome the challenges of future too

Summary

This chapter mainly discusses India's progress, pros and cons of defining poverty with the support of MDG report (2014) and estimates of planning commission's report (2013).From the analysis it is obvious that India is on track for achieving the first goal. The latest report pictures that with a faster decline in PHCR i.e. annual decline of 1.9 percentage points during 2004-12, compared to 0.7 percentage points during 1993-2004, the country has already achieved the MDG target. Though India boasts of high economic growth, it is shameful that there is still large scale poverty in India. Out of it's total population of more than one billion, 350 to 400 million people are still living below poverty line. Nearly 75 per cent of them are belongs to the rural areas. Most of them are daily wagers, landless labourers and self employed households. Economic growth, especially broad-based growth in agriculture and the rural economy, is a necessary and essential condition for sustainable poverty and hunger reduction. At the same time, priority action needs to be taken to reduce hunger directly. Hunger is not only an effect but also a cause of poverty. There is plenty of evidences which show that fighting hunger is an investment with high returns in growth and overall welfare and not just a moral imperative.

CHAPTER V

Summary of Major Findings, Suggestions and Conclusions

The Millennium Declaration of the United Nations set 2015 as the time- line for achieving most of the Millennium Development Goals (MDGs), which provide quantitative benchmarks for eradication of extreme poverty, hunger, illiteracy and diseases apart from achieving gender equality and empowerment of women, environmental sustainability and global partnership for development. The study mainly go ahead in terms of statistical measures of the given outcome indicators, outcome of the efforts that have gone into their operations so far, and the consequential projected outcome measures that are likely to emerge by 2015. The Millennium Declaration of 2000 consolidates and restates the commitments agreed during the preceding decade, and can be seen as the final stage of the Summit process. For the first time in a document of its kind, it stresses that, without policies and mechanisms to mobilize private and public resources on a much larger scale, the internationally agreed Millennium Development Goals (MDGs) for reducing poverty and hunger and for social and sustainable development cannot be achieved.

The Declaration is thus a starting point for renewed action in the twenty-first century.

SUMMARY OF MAJOR FINDINGS

- The all-India Poverty Head Count Ratio **(PHCR)** has declined by 15 percentage points from 37.2% in 2004-05 to 21.9% in 2011-12.
- Significant decline in **PHCR** has been observed in both rural and urban areas during this period as the rural poverty head count ratio declined by 16 percentage points from 41.8 percent to 25.7 percent and urban poverty declining by 12 percentage points from 25.7 percent to 13.7 percent.
- The lowest PHCR is for the State of Goa **(5.09 percent)** and the highest PHCR is for the State of Chattisgarh **(39.93 percent)**.
- Poverty Gap Ratio **(PGR)** has shown decline in rural and urban areas during 2004-05 to 2011-12. In rural areas, PGR declined from 9.22 in 2004-05 to 5.05 in 2011-12, while in urban areas the decline was from 6.08 to 2.7 during this period.
- In 2011-12, PGR in rural areas was above the corresponding all India figure in the States of Uttar Pradesh, Assam, Bihar, Manipur, Jharkhand, Odisha, Mizoram, Madhya Pradesh, Chattisgarh and Arunachal Pradesh.
- The recent trend of increase in poverty head count ratio as well as poverty gap ratio in some States i.e.

Arunachal Pradesh, Mizoram and Nagaland is quite worrying, indicating urgent need for more intensive and effective measures of poverty alleviation.

- The share of the poorest 20 percent population in terms of the monthly per capita consumption expenditure in total consumption in the rural areas has slightly increased from 9.6 percent in 1993-94 to 9.8 percent in 2009-10.

- In the urban areas the share of the poorest 20 percent population, declined from 8 percent in 1993-94 to 7.1 percent in 2009-10.

- The proportion of underweight children has declined by 3 percentage points during 1998-99 **(NFHS -2)** to 2005-06 **(NFHS-3)**, from about 43 percent to about 40 percent and at this historical rate of decline, it is expected to come down to about 33 percent only by 2015.

- As per **NFHS -3**, in India, one in every three children in the age group of 0-3 years is suffering from under weight

- Census 2011, reports nearly 89 million children in the age group 0-3 years and with the 40 percent prevalence of underweight, 35.6 million among them are underweight children.

- It may be noted that, the degree of decline for prevalence of stunting and underweight among children under 3 years of age, was very low i.e., less than one percentage point in both cases.

- The Census 2011 population results and the latest poverty head count ratio (2011-12) points out that, out of the 270 million poor people of India, 81 percent (217 millions) are from rural India.
- In all States except Punjab **(Rural: 7.66, Urban: 9.24)** rural poverty ratio was higher and the rural – urban gap in PHCR varied from 1 percentage point **(Uttar Pradesh - Rural: 11.62, Urban: 10.48)** to 29 percentage points **(Mizoram Rural: 35.43, Urban: 6.36)**.
- As per the historical trend, 23 States are likely to achieve their respective MDG target by 2015. Delhi, Bihar, Uttar Pradesh and Odisha are likely to miss their MDG target narrowly, and the States of Madhya Pradesh, Chattisgarh and Mizoram are likely to miss their MDG targets by huge margin.
- Among the major States, estimated per capita calorie intake **(Kcal)** per day in rural areas was highest in Punjab **(2223 Kcal)** and lowest in Jharkhand **(1900 Kcal)** in 2009-10 and in urban areas, the highest per capita calorie intake **(Kcal)** per day was reported in Odisha **(2096 Kcal)** and lowest in West Bengal **(1851 Kcal)**.
- Despite different achievements in India in development arena, still 350 to 400 million people remains below poverty line

SUGGESTIONS

- The private and public sectors have important roles to play in the battle against poverty and hunger. These roles are complementary, although each sector may have advantages in different areas.

- The public sector has a catalytic role, providing the public goods without which private initiative cannot flourish. However, the bulk of resources for agriculture and rural development will be mobilized by the private sector.

- Public investment is essential for agriculture and rural development especially in areas such as: agricultural research and extension; education; infrastructure and services; incentives and regulation for sustainable management of water and natural resources; decentralized social programmes in partnership with the private sector and civil society; market institutions; property legislation; food quality and food safeguards.

- Provision of credit facilities and expansion of market institutions as well as of appropriate infrastructure in the rural areas may help to reduce poverty and hunger to some extent.

- Microfinance and other rural financial institutions can mobilize substantial resources to enable poor people to become more productive by providing loans and mobilizing savings

CONCLUSION

Millennium Development Goals **(MDGs)** have helped in bringing a much needed focus and pressure on basic development issues, which in turn led the governments at national and sub national levels to do better planning and implement more intensive policies and programmes. Coming to India's achievement in respect of the MDGs, it is a mixed bag. For some indicators India is fast, that is, it has already achieved the target level well ahead of the dead line, like halving the percentage of population below the poverty line, for some indicators, India is expected to reach close to the target level by 2015 if not actually meet the target level like Ratio of girls to boys in primary and secondary education and tertiary education. For some other indicators it shows a sluggish improvement like reducing the child mortality.

Though India boasts of high economic growth, it is shameful that there is still large scale poverty in India, 350 to 400 million people are still living below poverty line. Nearly 75 per cent of them are belongs to the rural areas. Most of them are daily wagers, landless labourers and self employed households. There is plenty of evidences which show that fighting hunger is an investment with high returns in growth and overall welfare and not just a moral imperative. Civil organizations, especially international and national NGOs operating in developing countries like India, must commit themselves with renewed vigour to addressing the problems of hunger and rural poverty. They have important roles in mobilizing resources and providing technical services and advocacy. They may assume responsibility for monitoring performance against reaffirmed commitments, using score cards as a basis for measuring achievements. Economists can conduct an unending debate and related discussion about estimation and implementation of policies to remove abject poverty but the original fruits should be reached to the poor. Once Vivekananda postulated "we can't live happily as islands in a sea of poverty". A far more important and practical need today is to focus policy analysis on concrete measures for the benefit of poor, particularly the rural poor, who are more numerous but fail to catch as much attention as the urban poor.

Bibliography

- Ahluwalia, M.S., "Rural Poverty and Agricultural Performance in India" The Journal of Development Studies, Vol .14, No. 3, 1978,pp 298-323
- Ashwani Saith, "Production, Prices and Poverty in Rural India", The Journal of Development Studies, volume No.17, N0.2, January, 1981.
- Aurora G.S (2004), Poverty and Economic Reforms, The Social Concerns, Academic Foundations, New Delhi.
- Balisacan, Arsenio. M. "Rural Poverty in Philippinees" in Quibria M.G. (Ed) Rural Poverty in Developing Asia, VoL 2, Asian Development Bank, 1996.
- Bardhan, P.K.. "On the Incidence of Poverty in Rural India in the Sixties" in T.N. Srinivasan and P.K. Bardhan, op.cit., pp.264-280.
- Barton, C. (2005). Where to for Women's Movements and the MDGs? Gender and Development, pp. 25-35.
- Basu, A. M. (2007). Are Millennium Development Goals Relevant for Academic Research? Economic and Political Weekly, pp. 4235-4238.

- Bertha Nhlema Simwaka, S. T. (2005). Meeting Millennium Development Goals 3 and 5: Gender Equality Needs To Be Put On The African Agenda. British Medical Journal , pp. 708-709.
- Bhalla, S, (2003), India's Rural Economy: Issues and Evidence, Institute for Human Development Report, mimeo, New Delhi.
- Bhatty, I.Z., "Inequality and Poverty in Rural India" In T.N. Srinivasan and P.R.Bardhan, op.cit., pp.291-336.
- Chatterjee, B. (1998). Poverty in West Bengal: What Have We Learnt? Economic and Political Weekly, pp. 3003-3014.
- Datt et.al. (1992) "Growth and Redistribution Components of Changes in Poverty Measures: A de-composition with applications to Brazil and India in the1980s" Journal of Development Economics, 38, 1992.
- Dereon, Stephen and Krishan, "Vulnerability, Seasonality and poverty in Pramila. Ethopia", Journal of Development studies, Vol. 36, No.6, 2000.
- Ferreira et.al.(1996) "Inequality and Poverty in the Last Decade: Brazilian Income Distribution in the 1980s" in Victor Bulmor Thomas (Ed.) The New Economic Model in Latin America and its Impact on Income Distribution and Poverty, Macmillan, 1996.
- Fox, M. Louise et.al. (1993). "Poverty and Adjustment in Brazil: Past, Present and Future". In Lipton, Michael and Gaag, Jaquesvander (Ed) Op.Cit.

- Gautam Kumar Mitra, "Poverty, Land and Household Size, A Study of Andra Pradesh Districts", Margin, Vol.19, No.4, July-Sep. 1987, pp.51-54.
- Gooneratne's et.al (1984) "Poverty and Inequality in Rural Sri Lanka", in Khan, A.R. and Lee, Eddy (Ed) Poverty in Rural Asia, ILO, Geneva, 1977.
- Goverment of India (2012),12th plan Approach paper, Faster,More Inclusive and Sustainable Growth.
- Goverment of India(2013), Economic Survey 2013-14, Ministry of Finance,New Delhi
- Goverment of India(2013), Towards Achieving Millennium Development Goals India 2013, Social Statistics Division,New Delhi
- Government of India (2012). Twelfth Five Year Plan. New Delhi: SAGE Publications India Pvt Ltd. New Delhi 2012.
- Government of India (2013). SAARC Development Goals,India Country Report 2013.
- Government of India (2013). UPA Government Report to the People 2012-13. New Delhi: press information beuro.
- Government of India, (2005), The Millennium Development Goals Report,New Delhi.
- Government of India, (2010), The Millennium Development Goals Report, New Delhi

- Governmentof Indaia (1990). A profile of youth in india NFHS-1. Ministry of Health and Family Welfare, New Delhi
- Governmentof Indaia (1999). Gender equality women's empowerment in india NFHS-2. Ministry of Health and Family Welfare, New Delhi
- Governmentof Indaia (2006). Health and Living Conditions in Eight Indian Cities, NFHS-3. Ministry of Health and Family Welfare, New Delhi
- Guha Thakurtha,B.K., "Poverty in Calcutta, 1950-1972", Arthavijnana, Vo1.22, No.4, December 1980, pp.565-572.
- Himanshu, et.al. (2010), Towards New Poverty Lines for India. Economic & Political Weekly , 38-48.
- Jain, S. D. (1990). Rural Poverty and Its Alleviation in India: A Critical Scrutiny. Economic and Political Weekly , pp. 2165-2168.
- Jalan, Jyotsna and Ravallion, Martin."Spatial Poverty Traps ?", Policy Research Working Paper, 1862, World Bank, Washington D.e. 1997(a)
- John Butler CLRA (2009). Reaching MDGs in India. New Delhi: Vinodh banu, Excutive Director CLRA.
- Kannan, K. P. (1995). Declining Incidence of Rural Poverty in Kerala. Economic and Political Weekly, pp. 2651-2662.

- Khan, A. R. (2005). Employment and Millennium Development Goals: Analytics of the Linkage. The Bangladesh Development Studies , pp. 1-24.
- Krishnan, T. N. (1992). Population, Poverty and Employment in India. Economic and Political Weekly , pp. 2479-2489+2492-2497.
- Kumar, A, (Co-ordinator), "Rural Poverty in Orissa – A Case Study of Two Villages in the District of Puri", -Centre of Regional Studies, Utkal University, Bhubaneswar, 1982.
- Kurien, C.T. "Rural Poverty in Tamil Nadu", ILO, W.E.P Study,1980, pp.113-135
- Malik, Sohail J. "Poverty in Pakistan, 1984-85 to 1987-88", In Lipton, Michael and Gaag, J aquesvander (Ed) Including the Poor, World Bank International Food Policy Research Institute, 1993.
- Minhas, B.S., 'Rural Poverty, Land Redistribution and Development Strategy, in T.N. Srinivasan and P.K.Bardhan, (ed.) Poverty and Income Distribution in India. Statistical Publishing Society, Calcutta, 1974, pp.252- 263.
- Mitra, A. (1992). Growth and Poverty: The Urban Legend. Economic and Political Weekly , pp. 659-665.
- Parthasarathy, Sarveswara Rao, G.D. Rama Rao, "Character of Poverty Among Rural Poor - A Study of West Godawari District", in N.B. Sarveswara Rao and N.N. Deshpande.(ed.) E, Somaiya Publications, 1982, pp.30-47.

- Patwari, A. (2013). Millennium Development Goals and Child Undernutrition.Indian Pediatrics, volume 50.
- Raghav Gaiha, "On Measuring the Risk of Poverty in Rural India" in T.N. Srinivasan and Pranab K. Bardhan, op.cit., 1988, pp.219-261.
- Rathakrlshna. R., Banumati K. Parik and Shah N.C., "Levels of Living, Poverty and Liquor Consumption – A Study of Ahemmedabad Slums", Anvesak, Vol. XII, No.1, June 1982, pp. 57-84.
- Ravallion, M. (2000). Should Poverty Measures Be Anchored to the National Accounts? Economic and Political Weekly, Vol. 35, No. 35/36, pp. 3245-3247+3249-3252.
- Ravallion, M. (2002), Have We Already Met the Millennium Development Goal for Poverty. Economic and Political Weekly, 4638-4645.
- Sanyal, S.K., "Trends in Land-holdings and Poverty in Rural India" in T.N. Srinivasan and Pranab K. Bardhan, (ed.) op.cit, 1988, pp.121-153.
- Sarma, Perraaju, P., Dimensions of Rural Poverty, Daya Publishing House, Delhi, 1987.
- Scott, Christopher. D. "Mixed Fortunes: A Study of Poverty Mobility Among Small Farm Households in Chile, 1968-86", journal of Development Studies, Vo1.36, No.6, 2000

- Selden, J. M. (1992). Poverty and Inequality in China and India. Economic and Political Weekly, pp. 701-715.
- Sengupta, A. (2010). Human Rights and Extreme Poverty. Economic & Political Weekly, 85-93.
- Subbarao, N. K. (1991). Rural Poverty and Its Alleviation in India. Economic and Political Weekly, pp. 1482-1486.
- Subramanyam, S., "Poverty, Unemployment and Labour Force Participation", Margin, October 1982, Vol.15, No.1, pp. 58-70.
- Sudhakar Reddy S. and Gautam Kumar Mitra, "Poverty in Rural Medak Levels and Determinants", Margin, Vol.14, No.4, July 1982, pp.58-67.
- Sundaram, Dutt (2012), Indian Economy: Issues and Policy (67th edition), Chand Publication Private limited, 388-416
- Sundaram, K. and Suresh, D. Tendulkar, "Towards an Explanation of Inter regional Variations in Poverty and Unemployment in Rural India" in T.N. Srinivasan and Pranab K. Bardhan, (ed.) Rural Poverty in South Asia, Oxford University Press, New Delhi, 1988, pp. 316-362.
- Susanne Wymann von Dach, C. O. (2006). Will International Pursuit of the Millennium Development Goals Alleviate Poverty in. Mountain Research and Development, pp. 4-8.

- Thakur, D.S., "Estimation of Poverty in India – An Empirical Investigation", MARGIN, Vol.14. No. 4, October 1986, pp. 66-8.
- Thomas Pogge, M. S. (2013), New Millennium Development Goals; A New Version an Old List, Economic & Political Weekly , 23-25.
- Tiwari, M. (2007). Review Article: Chronic Poverty and Entitlement Theory. Third World Quarterly , pp. 171-191.
- UNDP, (2011), Human Development Report, Oxford University Press, New Delhi
- United Nations, (2005), The Millennium Development Goals Report, New york.
- United Nations, (2009), The Millennium Development Goals Report, New york.
- United Nations, (2010), The Millennium Development Goals Report, New york
- United Nations, (2013), The Millennium Development Goals Report, New york.
- United Nations, (2014), The Millennium Development Goals Report, New york.
- Vaidyanathan, Some Aspects of Inequalities in Living Standards in Rural India in T.N. Srinivasan and B.K Bardhan, op.cit., pp.215-241.

- Vishwa Mittar, "Income Distribution and Poverty in the Urban Informal Sector", Margin, Vol.18, No. 2, January 1986, pp. 29-41.
- Yao, Shujie."Economic Development and Poverty Reduction in China over 20 years of Reforms", Economic Development and Cultural Change, Vol. 48, No. 3, 2000.

Index

A

B

C

N

O

P

R

S

U

V

W

Y